Hazel was born in 1947. At the young age of two, she was dumped in a children's home in Nottingham because her birth mother thought that it would ruin her chances of going to America with her soldier boy, whom she had met just after the war. After that, Hazel's life changed forever. She has been candid with each word she has penned in this book, her first and only, now that she is 73 years old.

She has had more downs than ups, with violence and dangerous situations in her life, and remembers everything like it happened yesterday. She is very open about her life: the words she has written, which sometimes are very crude and to the point, describe every incident throughout her life.

She has still not found peace in her life up until this day and will always, as she puts it, remain broken.

Lots of Love Pauline

Enjoy

from the Author

H Longley.

I would like to dedicate this book to my daughter, Kelly Ann Williams.

She has known about most of my past life from a very young age and she was the one who gave me the strength and courage to finally put my story to paper.

Had it not been for her, I would have just kept my memories in my heart. Thank you, Kelly, for giving me the push that I needed.

Hazel Longley

WOUNDS THAT NEVER HEAL... 'BROKEN'

AUSTIN MACAULEY PUBLISHERS™

LONDON * CAMBRIDGE * NEW YORK * SHARJAH

A CIP catalogue record for this title is available from the British Library.

ISBN 9781398446595 (Paperback)
ISBN 9781398446601 (ePub e-book)

www.austinmacauley.com

First Published 2022
Austin Macauley Publishers Ltd®
1 Canada Square
Canary Wharf
London
E14 5AA

I would like to say a big thank you to Austin Macauley Publishers.

I am so grateful to all the team, the editors, the production department and anyone else who has been involved in producing this book about my life.

Thank you for putting up with my constant e-mails, my panic and my insecurities. I must have driven you all crazy. I am proud that you have stuck by me, knowing that all I had was a broken laptop, an old phone and no internet.

Once again, thanks guys for putting my life into a book and sticking with a little old lady like me who had no idea about the publishing world.

To the Start of My Memories

I would like to say a big thankyou to Kelly who has known about my life and is totally behind me in writing this book. It has taken me many years of thinking about it but as I am now over 70, I have had more colourful memories and events than a lot of people. God bless you Kelly, for telling me to do this.

And to my first love, wherever I go, I will always carry you with me. Take good care of your hurt, wherever you end up in life because it will fade, I promise you. Thank you for you.

Don't let life get in the way of your love story,
Mine did and it destroyed me.'

Introduction

I didn't have a childhood as such. I can only remember little snippets of growing up. I did not have any photos taken by my parents as a little girl, something parents always do, I suppose. Hardly any childhood memories except the basics and because I was an only child, I was always by myself and lonely and just made up my own little adventures like climbing trees and picking bluebells in the fields around me. I was not noticed much at home by either parent, I did not get cuddles or kisses and thought it was natural to live like that.

I didn't get kisses or cuddles or hugs and at that time, thought it was all normal. I think I loved my chickens in the garden more than I did my mum and dad and I was too young to know anything different. I have my memories of my childhood, but no proof that I ever existed and really felt that I did not belong anywhere at all. That about sums up my non-existent childhood and it was not until later on that a great shining light just happened and I started putting the pieces all together and that's when I was destroyed in so many ways. In fact, my whole life became one huge ticking time bomb just waiting to explode, so this book begins when my real life started, so this book may shock some people and bring tears to others but for me, it brought me a lifetime of heartache.

Prologue

Where do I start? Maybe at the beginning; in the middle or at the end? No, that would be too boring. So how about this beginning, confusion and frustration, rebellion and crazy and a return to sanity. That will just about cover my crazy life from age 11 until present day. My story began at the age of eleven years because before that I can't remember anything important happening in my life. I was an only child and a lonely child. I remember playing in the garden which had chickens. I remember collecting eggs from their nests every morning. I always got a Christmas stocking at the bottom of my bed on Xmas morning with simple wooden toys, apple, orange and that was it. I grew up learning how to play hopscotch, use a skipping rope and play with a spinning top. As well as that, I just went to my first school, learned my lessons and acted like the nice little girl that I was, until the age of 11 years. Then it all began to go downhill for a while, in fact, quite a long while. This is where the real part of my life begins, so go with the flow and travel the ups and downs of my life with me.

Chapter One
Bombshell

Being an only child, my life was uneventful. Nice parents, nice schools, happy holidays and nice friends at school. It was the early 1950s and everything was prim and proper and safe. In those days, kids could play in the fields, walk to school alone and not get accosted by perverts, and never get grabbed off the street while playing alone, which I often did. In fact, I had a pretty plain and ordinary life up until I started secondary school at age eleven. Everything was new, I was a little scared but I knew I had to buckle down and work hard and do lots more homework, that was until the day I had the biggest bombshell dropped on my head of all times, and where do you think it came from? My own bloody mother.

I had just come home from school and noticed she was being very quiet and then said she had something to tell me and asked me to sit down. I thought I had done something wrong at school and put my serious face on. She began by telling me that I was special, what that was supposed to mean, I don't know because I knew I was special because I was a pretty little blonde bombshell, even at my young age. She then carried on talking and told me I was special because I was chosen from lots of other children because she and Dad couldn't have a baby of their own naturally. Oh! For fucks sake, what did she do to get me then, go to a shop and buy me? (I can swear now because I'm 72 years old and allowed) Back in those days, I didn't know swear words existed so I just sat there with my mouth open looking at Mum. I remember asking where I did come from and was told that she and Dad had gone to a children's home, (What the bloody hell was one of them then?) Mum said it was a place where young unmarried girls go to have their babies when they were not married. It was considered shameful in the early '50s and '60s and if a girl wasn't married when she became pregnant, well, she had to give up her baby for adoption and that's what happened to me. Well, I was in a daze for a long time because, after the shock of what Mum had just told me had settled into the deepest part of my brain, I thought and thought and thought. Hang on, I've got another mother out there, the real one, the one who gave birth to me. Mum never mentioned anything again, and never told me any more about my life and I was expected to just carry on as normal (yeah, right).

There was one question I wanted to ask my mum though; did I come from Nottingham and she told me, yes, I did, 85, Queens drive in Nottingham city. That was it, the end of our little talk. Must admit though that I did put that address to the back of my mind (for now) and just carried on with my life of growing up, going to school and getting on with things. I think that at that time in my life, between the age of eleven and thirteen, I became or started to become a complete little bitch. I think the reason for that was the fact that I kept thinking about the fact that I had another mother out there somewhere – a real one, and that address kept popping up in my head as well. My head kept throwing up all these ideas, what if I started to sneak out at night while Mum and Dad were asleep, what if I stole some of my dad's threepenny bits from his savings tin (remember them things)? Well I do and my dad had lots of them so I used to get dressed, sneak downstairs, go and grab a handful of money and sneak out the front door with no idea where I was going but knew I wanted to find 85, Queens Drive. Well, considering it was around am in the early hours, I just started walking towards Nottingham. Big mistake as I got picked up by the local bobby, asked where a young girl like me was going and told him I was going to Nottingham.

'Oh no, you're not, girly, get in the car and I'm taking you home.'

Oh, Christ, I thought, *I'm going to get a smack for this.* So I told Mr Policeman that if he took me to my door, I would creep back in as it wasn't locked and go straight to bed and please don't tell my mum and dad or I would be in trouble.

He looked at my little innocent face and fell for it. He watched me go in and then drove off. I did the running away thing for months, walking the streets, not getting anywhere until one late night, I was rumbled, as I was just going out the door, by my dad who was standing behind me. *I am now in deep shit,* I thought as I turned 'round to look at him.

He asked me where I was going and I said I didn't know and that I was sorry. Dad was a very gentle, quiet man and told me never to do it again. Promised him I wouldn't, gave him his money back and went to my room. Didn't get the bollocking I thought I would get, went to my room, sat on my bed and thought to myself, *you know what, I will wait until I'm older*, and with that, I went to sleep.

1960 was the year I discovered BOYS! I was 13 years old and my mum had never told me anything about boys, the birds and bees or anything else. Things like that were never spoken about in those early days as it was all considered dirty and my mother never even told me about menstruation. I can always remember the first time I started my period. I was in the bathroom cleaning my teeth when I felt a trickle of something running down the inside of my leg. I screamed, shouted for my mum and yelled that I was bleeding to death. She took one look, vanished into her bedroom and came back with an elastic belt to go 'round my waist with a plastic hook at the front and one at the back, then she handed me a cotton pad with a loop on the front and back. She then put the pad between my legs hooking the loops to the front and back (does anyone remember those prehistoric ugly fucking things?). When I put my knickers on and got dressed, I was walking bandy-legged like a bloody cowboy. On the way out the door, Mum turned to me and said, 'You are a woman now.' End of sex education lesson. The rest I had to find out for myself; at school and with boys and wow, did I have fun! Apart from doing my schoolwork, I also became a favourite with the boys and there was quite a bit of exploring that was being done (I call it groping). There would be my hand, down some good-looking boy's trousers and same boy with his hand up my skirt having a quick feel. It turned out to be real fun but never went any further than that, although I do remember the handsome looking boy who worked in the local garage that I had to walk past to get to school every day. His name was Rex and he always had eyes for me and I loved the way he smelled of car oil and grease, and also the fact that he was eighteen. I ended up sneaking into the woods with him, finding out a lot more about what the word "sex" really meant. Must admit that was a really exciting time for me. I was 13 years old and doing well in school and was happy at home. One night, I didn't feel very well before I went to bed. I had quite a bad stomach ache that didn't go away and felt a bit sick. Well, me being me, I went downstairs and got the old-fashioned Medical Encyclopaedia and took it up to my bedroom. Mum thought I was being dramatic and told me it was probably something to do with my periods. I sat in bed reading through it anyway. I went through nearly every page of that book and all my symptoms pointed to appendicitis. Didn't sleep well and got up the next morning feeling like shit!

Didn't eat breakfast, put my uniform on and walked about a mile to school. I really did not feel well but went to school anyway. Went into assembly and about halfway through, I had to walk out to go to the toilet. Didn't even make it there, went through the cloakroom, stood against the wall and was very sick all over the floor. That was so embarrassing for me. The nurse was sent for and I was taken into the little medical room there. I told her how I felt and she wrote a letter to my doctor and told me to go straight down and give it to him. It wasn't a long walk and I went straight there.

In those days, your local doctor's surgery was the front of a house with only one doctor and you just sat on a wooden chair and waited, which was not long this time as I was called in straight away. I was examined yet again and another letter was written and he told me to go home and tell my mum to take me straight to the hospital. My doctor was so sweet and although the envelope was sealed which he gave me, I pretty much knew what he had written about me. Feeling sick and looking grey, I got home, handed my mum the letter and told her that our doctor had told me she had to take me straight to the hospital. She gave me a funny look like she was pissed off that I had interrupted her day but put on her coat and guess what, she walked me to the fucking bus stop to wait for the bus. It was five miles to Nottingham city; I had been sick again, my skin looked grey but she took me to the hospital on the sodding bus. I knew what was wrong with me, I believed in that old fashioned medical dictionary and the symptoms and I've known for years since that every person knows their own body and how they feel and the medical profession should listen to them more. I was learning about my body as I started growing up and I knew I had "appendicitis". (Hello, all you thick people out there, Mum included, periods, my arse.) Anyway, got to the hospital and I was told to lie on a trolley and a big chubby doctor poked around my tummy and within two hours I was being wheeled into the theatre to have an operation. I was very scared, felt very alone but guess what? Yes, you've guessed it! I had my appendix out as it was ready to burst. See, I was right, just by reading a tatty old medical dictionary and no one believed me. I was in the hospital for 14 days and was in a ward full of old ladies. It was bloody horrible and I was glad to get home to rest up before going back to school and I was really proud of my scar. I knew I had a bad appendix but no one believed me. Anyway, life carried on. I was still a rebel and started going out with boys. My last two years at school were uneventful. I took my last exams, didn't pass any of them (I didn't give a toss) but I did get the instinctive feeling that my mum was a bit disappointed in me, and so the school found me a job at Boots warehouse in town, filling orders for the shops. Left school at 15 years and felt really grown up (about bloody time). It was around this time that I thought my mum was ashamed of me and she thought of it as a duty to bring me up not out of love (didn't feel like I got much of that anyway) but out of a duty to perform like she was a real mother to me and none of the bond which happens between a real birth mother and child. Well, that wasn't my fault, I didn't ask to be chosen! I still felt like I was rebellious. I was really glad I was going to start work because it meant I could get away from Mum for a longer time each day and have more freedom. I began wearing miniskirts, high heels and dyed my hair platinum blonde. I was not the flavour of the month with my parents but I didn't give a toss. I decided to get out there and enjoy myself and look for a boyfriend and boy, did I do that. Started work and enjoyed it as it got me away from home all day, and I also discovered where the local dance hall was. It was the dance hall, in Ilkeston.

Well, my friend and I had a fantastic time that night. You couldn't buy alcohol, it was soft drinks only but all we did all night was dance to all the rock and roll music and I must admit that even today, after all these years, all the music then was so much better than some of the shit that is put out there today. A good night was had by all and my friend from work came with me and we caught the bus to my house as she was staying at my house for the night. We sat at the front of the bus and there were two boys sitting at the back and slowly but surely they edged their way towards the front and ended up sitting behind us and started chatting us up. Well, we enjoyed that and lo and behold! When it came to our stop, the boys got off too. Have to admit, I did like the look of one of them and he wanted to kiss me goodnight. Me being me, I did not hesitate. He looked like Elvis Presley. My hero! Jet black quiffed hair, long sideburns, black tight jeans and a topcoat down to his knees, finished off by Beetle Crushers. (Remember them, anyone?) God, he had the most beautiful lips I had ever seen. Being pushed up against the bus shelter, I enjoyed the very first tender, soft kiss of my life. My legs went weak, I saw stars and I just melted into his arms. They always say a girl will always remember her first kiss and I certainly will remember that one for a long time to come. He had beautiful dark eyes and stared at me for the longest time. I did get my breath back eventually and he asked if he could see me the following night. I did not hesitate and said yes and we arranged to meet at the bottom of my road the following night. I and my friend went to my house. I thought it was really funny because she got the ugly one and he didn't kiss great and she was not impressed at all. She had not made plans to see him again. Hahaha. I took the piss out of her that night but the butterflies stayed in my tummy all night and I could not stop thinking about my date with him the following night. I really did fancy him like crazy and could not wait. Told my mum the next day that I had a date that night after work and she did not seem bothered. I didn't give a toss, to be honest, because if she had said no, I would have gone out anyway.

Chapter Two

First Love

I was so looking forward to tonight. I made sure I looked nice, make-up perfect, mini skirt, stockings and suspender belt (yes folks, girls wore them all the time in those days), high heels and backcombed hair which I sprayed with about half a tin of hairspray. Must admit, looking in the mirror, I didn't look too bad. It was 1962 and I was 15 years old and going on my first date, excited or what. As I was leaving, Mum turned to me and said, 'Be home by ten.'

'Okay,' I promise.

Can't believe I've just been given my first curfew. Oh well, that's parents for you, especially mine. Couldn't wait to get away and as I walked to the bottom of my road and neared the main road, some car headlights flashed in my direction so I squinted at the window shield and there he was, sitting behind the wheel of this car. Oh My God! He was just sitting looking at me and smiling. He was only one year older than me and should not have been driving but hey, that added to the excitement of it all. I got in and off we drove. He didn't ask me where I wanted to go, he just drove. I knew in the back of my mind that he was looking for a quiet spot and we certainly found one of those because we ended up in a farmer's field. It was all countryside in those days. None of these high-rise flats and takeaways, just fields and woods and so we ended up in a field. I seemed to think that was a nice place to be on that night because I fancied him like mad and was glad I was alone with him. We just looked at each other and then he asked if I would feel more comfy in the back seat. Tell you what, I did not hesitate and then we were together and the tender kisses started, making me feel weak at the knees. Well, I was putty in his hands and from kissing it went to exploring each other and feeling warm and great and slowly, he started to pull my panties down and I didn't stop him but had to mention that I was on my period. He told me not to worry and it didn't matter as he would be careful. I believed him and I was so far gone with the feelings I had for him, I didn't care. He was tender and gentle and loving and I was not scared and he made love to me that night and he took my virginity. He was the first and although it hurt a little, I was completely in motion with him and really enjoyed being close to him (you know who you are, if you are reading this). We were so complete and so entwined that I felt there was no other way to be. He was gentle and loving and completely kissable. It felt like we were never going to part, our bodies as one and I never wanted it to end, but it had to eventually. That first love and that first union was something I have and will not forget to my dying day. I knew it had to come to a stop though as I had a curfew (don't forget), so we sorted ourselves out and got back into the front seats and we were ready to go, only we weren't. My first love tried to start the car and it didn't budge. We were bogged down in this bloody field and the car would not budge. Well, imagine this scenario, my boyfriend had to go look for the farmer who turned up with his tractor and hooked up the car and pulled us out of the muddy field and back onto the road. Christ, how red-faced we both were but the farmer just grinned. He knew and he knew that we knew what we had been up to. Well, I got home just before my curfew and all was well. After that, we could not get enough of each other. We saw each other all the time and I did not want any other boys. He would meet me from work and we would go out at night and he even came home to meet my mum and dad. They accepted him and we were always in my front room just kissing or groping and being sexy with each other.

The place where I had first my first kiss with Stephen

We became an item after that. We saw each other all the time and had sex whenever we had the chance. Deep in my heart, I thought that if I got pregnant, I would love to have a baby with him because he was the only one I wanted to get pregnant with and would be proud to carry his baby (yes, I had by then found where babies come from, no thanks to my mother or the school). There was never any sex education from anyone in those days. The less it was spoken about the better. It was all so secretive. I thought in my immature mind that if I eventually got myself pregnant then it would give me the chance to get away from my mum and dad and the house too and I really wasn't getting much attention from them anyway. Well, I just kept going to work every day and meeting my dream boy after work. At that time, I was having trouble with my periods, in fact, I had missed three so decided to call and see my doctor on the way home. Doctor M was very nice and gave me an internal examination and then said very quietly that I was pregnant. Told him I would break the news to my mum when I got home and just then, in that surgery room, on the examination table, I looked down at my stomach which was flat, put my hand on my stomach and kept it there in a protective sort of way. The feelings going through me then were happy, proud, in awe! And absolutely shit scared of how I was going to tell my mother. In fact, I didn't tell her that day or the day after, but then on the third day, I came home from work and sat at the table waiting for my tea and noticed that Mum was very quiet. When she gave me my food, she looked at me and told me that she had a visit from Doctor M and he told my mum everything. All she said to me was, 'How could you get in the family way just after leaving school? Your dad and I were expecting you to pay us back for a few years for everything we have done for you since you were little and we bought you up and spent all our money on you and now this is how you repay us?'

I swear to God, that's what she said to me. It made me feel like I owed them something for all the years I had been growing up.

'You will have to get married now you know, and the sooner the better before you start to "show".'

I was by now just 16 years old and my lover boy was 17. Told Mum I was sorry (wasn't really) and got dressed up to go meet my man and tell him the news. We met up at his mum's house and I told him I was going to have his baby. His mum was more understanding and said after we got married, we could go live with her and his dad. *Cool,* I thought, at least I could get away from my parents at last and my man was over the moon and happy. Mum didn't lose too much time sorting me out. The quicker the better, I reckon, she thought. She bought me a short silk wedding dress, cream coloured (well I wasn't a virgin, was I? I had been deflowered in her eyes and she was ashamed of me.). Well, we were married in the local church in Kimberley, and the only people there were my mum and dad, my godparents and the groom's mum and dad and sister. That was how quick it was. We all went to the big Co-Op store in town and had just an ordinary dinner, then with my new husband, we went to share his mum and dad's house. Wow! I was actually married and wore a wedding ring. I was three months pregnant and was carrying my new husband's baby inside me. We were both very happy and I can even remember where my baby was conceived. In a field full of buttercups opposite his mum and dad's.

At that very moment, three months before, everything was perfect. It was a warm day and we lay in the grass for the longest time and when we made love we came in unison and I just knew something magical had just happened. I also knew that my boyfriend had felt it too and now here I am, married, pregnant, starting to make arrangements to attend ante-natal classes and keeping my appointments with my doctor. Everything was going perfect. My husband was working as a coalman, delivering coal to people's houses from a lorry and I just got fatter. I still visited my parents but they were a little bit offish with me but pleasant enough. Now I was married, they were a bit happier because the neighbours didn't talk and I hadn't bought shame to the street. It went fine living with his mum and dad but as I got bigger and more pregnant, little did I know that my mum and dad had been in the process of buying another house just around the corner from where I grew up, and as I visited them quite often, I was very surprised when they asked us to move into the house with them just before the baby was born. It was much bigger with a lovely back bedroom to set up for a baby and Mum even found someone who sold her a baby pram. It was a silver cross and was purple and cream. It was beautiful and as everything was coming together for the arrival of our baby, Mum took to knitting baby clothes and getting everything ready for the birth, which would not be long now.

She seemed to be a bit happier for us now but I think it was because she had moved a little away from the street where she lived and didn't feel so embarrassed by it all. If anyone can remember the television series *Call the Midwife*, well, my life and pregnancy were just like that in real life back in the old days when everything was so basic but so fun. Yes, we had to struggle to make ends meet with food and baby things and stuff like that but we just did it and it was all okay. Settled in yet again in another house, life carried on as normal. My husband went to work, I helped Mum around the house and kept up my ante-natal appointments and when I was in my ninth month, I looked like I was carrying a football in my stomach. You must remember, I was barely sixteen and skinny and had beanpole legs, small boobs and thought to myself, *I'm still only a child myself.* Must admit, I was excited but scared at the same time. Didn't know what was going to happen but was about ready for it now as I was waddling around like a duck with this huge belly that was about ready to pop. One morning, I woke up with a slight dull ache in my stomach, kept wanting to wee but didn't think much of it as Mum had decided to come on the bus to the hospital with me that day as I had my ante-natal clinic. I began to feel very uncomfortable and could not seem to be able to sit still on the bus but stuck it out and finally arrived at the hospital. In ante-natal, I was examined and told I was to stay in hospital as I was in labour. Jesus Christ, this was it. D-day, I was having a baby and did not realise that I must have been in labour on the bus. Mum was sent home, I was put to bed on a ward and given a glass of the most disgusting stuff in my life, castor oil laced with orange juice.

'That will help you give birth quicker.'

Yes, I thought, *you bloody bitch, you are trying to fucking poison me. I did not want that. And NO more… Pleaseeeee!!!*

I didn't mean to think nasty things like that about the nurse, who was really nice, all dressed in her starched white apron and crisp white nursing cap. After about two hours of laying in bed feeling uncomfortable, the nurse popped to see me again, to examine me. She gave me an internal and told me I was fully dilated and about to give birth. I was pushed in my bed, down a corridor to a white-tiled delivery room. I was told that if I felt like I wanted to push, 'Don't! Not yet.'

I was told to climb up on a table and I lay down. And with that, it all got very clinical. My tummy was covered in a blanket but my legs were put up into stirrups and I was told that the next time I felt like pushing, I could. Chin on my chest and push as hard as I could until the pain died down. I did as I was told but I was not prepared for the pain. I felt like I was being ripped apart. The pain was so incredible, there are no words. I remember screaming, swearing, telling the nurses to piss off and not to touch me, and I kept pushing every time I felt I had to, then a nurse said, 'Come on, my dear, I can see the head, just one last push, there's a good girl.'

I did as I was told and finally, I felt the relief of sorts. The next urge to push and my baby was born. I heard a tiny cry and was told I had a little girl. The feeling of pain instantly left me and I forgot all about it when my baby daughter was handed to me wrapped in a little warm blanket. I just gazed at this tiny little human being and was completely in awe. She was like a little doll and had the thickest mop of jet-black hair I had ever seen. She weighed in at 5 pounds 4 ounces. That was tiny, and she looked just like her daddy and nothing like me. It felt wonderful and when the nurses put her to my breast and taught me how to feed her, it was the most wonderful feeling in the world. I was taken to a ward to settle in for the ten-day rest policy, and later on, in the day, my husband came to see his new daughter. We both cried and I still could not believe that this tiny human being had come from inside me when I was so small myself, still a child basically at sixteen. Both families came to visit but soon the ten days were up and we took our new daughter home back to my parents' house. It was easy settling in and I really got into a nice routine with the nurse paying me follow-up visits for a while. Was getting on quite well, learning how to breastfeed our daughter, settling into a routine. My husband went to work and I was really happy and then my life was turned upside down in just one afternoon. It was a normal Sunday afternoon and we had all had Sunday dinner. I was holding our baby, wrapped in a shawl and everything was peaceful. Suddenly, there was a knock on the door in the front room, I got up with the baby in my arms to go answer it. When I opened the door, there was this beautiful blonde-haired woman standing there and next to her was a young girl, maybe a bit older than me, with long blonde hair. This woman looked at me and asked if I knew who she was. 'No!' I said. 'I didn't.'

Well, she said she was my real mother and had come all the way from America to find me. I just stood there like a bloody statue, with my mouth open. 'Oh!' she said. 'And this is your sister Sandra.' This older version of me started to walk up the passage to my mum's back door but Mum wouldn't let her in. She told me she was my birth mother and was living in Spain now as my stepdad was at the air force base there.

Well, you could have knocked me sideways with a bleeding feather. I looked at my husband and he looked at me and my mum seemed to be angry and going purple in the face. My real mother passed me a piece of paper with her name and address on it and decided to leave before my adopted mum smacked her one. That was one very confusing, and surprising afternoon plus, I had the awkward job of telling hubby about my situation from age eleven. After everyone had calmed down, we all carried on as normal, but I must admit I did keep that bit of paper. As the baby grew, Mum seemed to be a little agitated about us being in her house. It was still another small house and we kept getting under each other's feet so I and hubby had a little talk with his brother who lived in a place called Newthorpe Common, near Eastwood, Nottingham and they said they had a spare room in their council house we could move into while we were waiting for the council to give us something. It was a good move, to be honest because I was getting a bit pissed off with my mum always trying to butt in and tell me what to do. She had never had kids so she did not know how to take care of my daughter like I did and I also think she was a bit jealous because I gave birth to a baby and she couldn't and didn't know what it felt like. Well tough, I thought and just could not wait to get away from her. Life was good at our new lodgings. Everyone got on together, I looked after our baby girl who was growing by the minute and hubby had a job. We stayed with them for about a year and finally we got word that we were going to be given a cottage temporarily, then move to a council house. This was great news. I know it was a temporary cottage, one of four in a row, and was due to be torn down soon, still, it was a private place of our very own. Couldn't wait to move in and could not wait to tell my husband that I had missed my period. 'Whoops.' We both never thought about birth control, but it didn't matter, now that I had one baby, I knew what to expect so I was happy. We both went to look at the cottage. It was tiny, old, two bedrooms and had an outside toilet. I was gobsmacked but if it meant us getting a council house, then I would stick it out. Our little girl was nearly a year old, and the few belongings we had, I piled onto the pram and pushed it up the hill about a mile away with our little girl in the pram as well as everything else. You have to remember that I was just pregnant again, hubby at work and me doing everything, but I was happy because we would have privacy as well as having to take a torch with us every time we used the toilet. 'God help me.'

The family gave us bits of furniture and I made curtains for the kitchen. We settled in and we were very happy. Must admit, it was a creepy little place with a cottage on either side. Bushes and trees were all around us and now I could see why the council had condemned them. Still, if we stayed put then we would get a council house quicker. We stayed put and the love of my life was on shift work, so when he was on afternoons, it was spooky, and when he was on nights, I was absolutely bloody terrified. Noises outside intensified, the wind blew the bushes too hard, and being alone with a little daughter, and pregnant as well scared me shitless.

I was always happy when hubby came home from work and wondered just how long we would have to live there before we got a move. Well, I got fatter and frumpy and was just about ready to pop. One night, I had a really bad stomach-ache and got the torch and went to the bloody outside lav. Luckily, my husband was home and as I sat on the loo, I felt something pop and suddenly felt very wet, and it wasn't wee. Holding my hand under my belly, I got back into our tiny falling apart cottage and told hubby to phone for an ambulance. He had to go up the road to the phone box to do that. (Mobile phones hadn't been invented then.) Finally, the ambulance turned up and carted me off to the hospital to give birth and my husband looked after our first daughter, who was just under a year old. I really was a glutton for punishment, wasn't I? Next time I will keep my legs closed more often ('course I will), hahaha. This time, I did not enjoy the birth at all. The delivery room was cold, I was left on my own, ignored by the damn nurses and they were or seemed very cold towards me. At the last minute when I could not wait any longer, I started pushing. I swear that is a feeling any woman giving birth cannot ignore.

'I'm going to push now,' I screamed, and I did just that. I knew I was ready so fuck 'em! Oh, they all came running then. I didn't have my legs in stirrups, there was no time. This time it really bloody hurt so they told me to breathe in the gas and air. Helped a bit, but not a lot and I did not have this with baby one as she came within two hours and seemed to just skid out. Finally, the head was out and they told me I had another little girl. After she was cleaned up and wrapped in a shawl, they bought her to me. I looked at her in my arms and thought, *Christ, she's nothing like the first one.* She was a big baby, and she was almost bald except for the blonde fuzz covering her head. I was not impressed at first but loved her just the same. Had to stay for the ten-day rule as was in those days then I went home. Was so happy to be out of there, I felt contented at home. Life went on and I really thought that we would get a council house soon. These shitty cottages were bound to be pulled down soon, and I carried on bringing up two daughters while he went back to work. Daughter one was around two years old and so pretty and helped me do things around the cottage but I couldn't quite get to grips with daughter two who screamed constantly, was never satisfied with any cuddling I gave her but took milk well and put on weight. It was very frustrating for me. People have to remember, I was just sixteen when I had my first baby, seventeen when I had my second, and was thrown into motherhood so quick, I had no time to grow up myself. Don't get me wrong, I loved my husband with all my heart and will love him until I die, I loved my two little young ones but I began to feel restless after a few months and I don't know why, I felt like a gypsy, wanted to travel but didn't know where to, but deep down I think I did. I still at the back of my mind wanted to find my birth mother and I had always kept that little bit of paper she gave me with her address on it and I started to hatch a plan to try to find her yet again. I made a plan in my mind that if I could find someone to give me a lift to Dover to catch the ferry to Calais, from there I could get a train to Paris and go to the British Embassy there and show them the address I had for my mother and ask them if they would phone her to come and fetch me. My heart was beating so fast. I felt sick with nerves, I was shaking! I knew I had to take this chance, but didn't want to. I loved my husband so much, but only had about five minutes to make a move before he came home from work and I also had to make the decision quickly to leave one child behind. I had decided to scoop up my firstborn as she was the one who was toddling about, I threw a few nappies into a bag, a couple of bits of fruit, and packed cushions around my second child on the sofa, who was screaming her head off. Her daddy would be home any minute but I had to go, so I ran to the road, holding my little girl's hand and getting in a car with someone I hardly knew. I was crying so much. I really should not have done it, I know but I wanted to find my real mother and told my little girl we were going on a big adventure, even though I was crying and my heart was breaking. I kept thinking that I was a horrible mother; "I had left my baby!" What sort of cruel bitch does that?

Something in my head was telling me that I should not leave but my heart told me that I needed to meet up with my real birth mother because when I first saw her, there were so many questions I needed to ask her but didn't have a chance so I decided to keep going. How this journey was going to end, I had no idea but we drove through the night and my daughter slept until we arrived at Dover Docks on the coast. I had a little money, so I gave my little girl some chocolate I had with me and told her I would get her some breakfast once we were on the ferry to France. She was so good, bless her, and didn't complain. I found a ferry to take us both to Calais and I was so very frightened, confused and lost. I worked out that I had just enough money for a one-way ticket on the boat to Calais, and from there, just a one-way ticket to Paris where I would find the British embassy and explain my situation. This journey turned out to be a journey from hell. I only had three terry-towelling nappies with me and no money for food to feed my child. Each time my daughter soiled her nappy on the journey, I had to take her into one of the toilets and change her and wash the soiled nappy out in the sink and hope to God it would dry whilst in my bag. My head was full of guilt and remorse for what I was doing but this feeling inside me kept driving me on. When we boarded the train to Paris, my daughter was crying because she was hungry, and as we both sat opposite an old man in one of the compartments, he could somehow tell that I was struggling. For god's sake, I was only seventeen and now, very confused. The man asked if there was anything wrong and I told him I was going to the British embassy in Paris, so I could find my birth mother but had no food to give to my daughter. He was very kind and offered my little girl a sandwich from his case. *Such a kind man*, I thought and thanked him profusely. Well, when we arrived in Paris, it was evening and dark and I was scared of all the bright lights and noise. I held my daughter's hand tightly as I could see there were many dangers on these streets. We walked and walked, not knowing where I was going, but I finally saw a police car and went and asked for help. Hoping he could help me, I asked him where the British embassy was and when he looked at how cold my little girl was, he offered to drive us there. We arrived and I asked the guard on the door if I could speak to someone inside as we had come all the way from England to find my real mother and that we were cold and my little girl was hungry. I don't think I would have coped mentally for much longer. We were taken in and I asked if I could see someone to help me get in touch with my mother and sister who lived in Spain. I gave the piece of paper to the gentleman and asked if he could try and trace them and phone them and could we please have a warm drink for me and my young daughter as we were thirsty and hungry because we had been travelling for a long time. We were given a hot chocolate each and felt so much better. For what seemed an age, there was quiet and my little one had fallen asleep on my knee. Finally, the gentleman came back and told me that they had been able to reach my real mother, and she had given instructions that she would accept me and get me to Spain, but said she would not accept my child. What was this woman thinking! I was part of her by blood, my child was part of me and her by blood, in fact, this was her granddaughter but she was adamant, she would only take me. Something inside me snapped. I cried, I screamed, I rocked back and forth in my chair and told the man that I was not going without my child and was so angry that I told the man to tell her on the phone to fuck off and that she was a bitch and I hated her. 'You bloody tell her that right now.'

They obviously did that and I calmed down a little. I was a wreck, my little girl was tired and I asked the man what I was supposed to do because I had no money and no way of getting back home. These people were really nice and they said we could stay until the morning, gave us something to eat and gave us a little room where we could get some sleep. To be truthful, I wanted to go home, realising what a stupid cow I had been, thinking I could do this on my own at seventeen. To be honest, I didn't even think I had a husband and baby to go back to. The next morning, I was told that I would be given a voucher from the embassy, allowing me and my little girl to travel all the way back to England. All I had to do was show it on the train, then the ferry and even the bus from Nottingham to our house. It would all be paid for, we just had to get home. Someone had made up some sandwiches for us and we were driven to the train station and put on a train to Calais, where we caught the ferry back to Dover, got a train to Nottingham and from the train station, got a bus back to near where we lived. It was amazing really just how kind these people had been to us.

My heart was thumping out of my chest, I did not know what I was going to find when I got back to the cottage. It was all in darkness when I turned the corner but my next-door neighbour had his lights on. I knocked pensively on the door next to mine. I was in luck, he had my door keys and let me in. He helped me to get a nice warm coal fire going so it didn't take long to get warm and he also heated some soup up for my little darling who was starving. I warmed up by the fire and slowly got the full story from the man next door. I was bloody horrified by what I heard. He told me that my other baby was being looked after by my father-in-law and the family, my husband had come back to the cottage alone, turned on the gas in the oven in our kitchen and knelt down and put his head inside to try and gas himself because of the situation. It was by sheer luck that the man next door had gone into our cottage to see if hubby was okay and found him unconscious. An ambulance was called and now my husband was in the hospital, fighting for his life, and it was all my fucking fault. *Oh my god, what have I done*, I thought to myself. I'm to blame and with that, I just crumpled into a heap onto my living room floor. I asked the man who found him to phone my father-in-law to ask if he would come and take my daughter away to his house to feed her and let her sleep. She was so exhausted, bless her and didn't understand what was going on at all. Now it was just a matter of time before my hubby's dad turned up and the butterflies were churning in my tummy. Eventually, he turned up and I faced him and there were no words. I could tell he was angry and I asked him if he could take our little girl and keep her warm and feed her up as she had lost some weight during this long bloody damn journey I had taken but regretted. All he said was, 'You better go and see your husband in the hospital,' and with that, he took my little girl by the hand and walked out the door.

God, how he must have hated me and I felt so ashamed for what I had done. I had decided to get a few hours' sleep as it was night time yet again and I was exhausted beyond belief. Morning came, sooner than I wanted it to but I knew what I had to do. I had a quick wash down (no bathroom where we lived). Managed to make myself look decent and realising what I had to face, I began my journey by bus to the hospital. Arriving at the hospital, I was directed to a ward. In the early days, the wards were long with rows of beds on either side and Matron had her desk in the middle of the ward and she sat there, all starched

29

uniform, prim and proper and stern looking. I walked up to her and told her I had come to visit my husband and gave his name. She looked down her nose at me, standing there in my mini skirt and orange fluffy sixties coat. She led me to his bed and walked away. My first love was lying on his side as I walked towards his bed, and he looked straight at me. He started crying and I was crying uncontrollably. I went up to him and held him in my arms, so happy to hold him tightly, feeling him, smelling his smell, but would he forgive me??? He stared at me and the only words he said to me were that he loved me and could we stay together and would I get the children, take them home so he could get out of the hospital and come home. I nodded, promised him I would never leave again, what I did was stupid and told him that I really did love him and that I was sorry for what I had done to him. We just held on to each other and it felt like we were the only people on that ward and nothing else mattered. I stayed for as long as possible, then was told visiting time was over and asked to leave. I made a promise to the love of my life that I would be waiting for him and we would be together again. We kissed, just like that first kiss when I was fifteen, (yes, even today at seventy-two, the same butterflies swirled within me) but more about that later. His dad brought the two girls home to our cottage and I fell into home life once again and felt really stupid for what I had done in the first place. I had to wait a couple more days before the hospital released my husband and one day, there he was, walking through the door. We held each other tightly, never wanting to let the other go, but I was reeling from what I had done and the damage I had caused, and also the fact that I had very nearly lost the love of my life. We made up big time, and both girls were happy to be a family unit again. He was very forgiving and I did my very best to be the perfect mother and wife, even at seventeen. We made love all the time, in fact, we went at it like rabbits, any chance we got. We both needed this intimacy and love to bring us closer together. Our life carried on, I was forgiven and eventually, we had a letter from the council, telling us that the cottages were being pulled down and we were being offered a three-bedroomed council house, just down the road from where I grew up. Wow! We were so excited and we had toughed it out for so long in the little dilapidated shithole we were living in, we jumped at the chance. We were told we could move in within the week, so we started packing everything up and bit by bit, loading it onto the pram along with my second daughter, and my first who was walking now as she was just over two years old, started moving into our new home. The council house was new and we were just planning what colours to paint every room with. Our family were giving us items of furniture, and we made a lovely burning open coal fire. Everything started to come together. We both had put my little escapade behind us and we worked hard on the house. We were very happy and contented. We had been there quite a while until another bombshell hit. Hubby came home one day and told me he had been laid off and now had no job. It could not have come at a more inconvenient time. We had a little girl two years of age, a baby of six months and now my hubby had to go on the dole. Oh well, we would cope somehow. All the family would and did rally 'round, helping out with food and helping with the bills and stuff until hubby got his first lot of dole money so I know it would all work out fine. Life carried on as normal and we put the past behind us. We got on with our lives and then the unthinkable happened! I missed a PERIOD! Oh Christ, no, not now, not again. Kept quiet about it but not for long because I missed two more. I went to the doctor and he confirmed it. I was ecstatic and when I told hubby, he was over the moon plus gobsmacked. I went to my local ante-natal clinic in Kimberley and told them that this time I was going to have my baby at home with a midwife to help me. After the bad second experience, I had in the hospital with my baby, there was no way I was going through that again and anyway in the sixties, women were having babies at home all the time and it was the natural thing to do unless there were complications, so we had both made our mind up, this child was going to be born at home and that was that. My mother didn't seem to approve of me being pregnant so soon after my second daughter, and reckoned I was popping babies out like peas in a pod. I didn't care what she thought anymore. We were both happy and looking forward to having this baby in our new home. I didn't realise it then but by the time this baby came along, I would have all three in nappies and realised that I had my work cut out for me. Well, the family started knitting, but I had saved loads of baby clothes from the other two little ones so just about had everything sorted. The days and months passed quickly and I and hubby carried on living and loving and being happy. We had a visit from the midwife who would be looking after me, she turned up in her uniform on a bike (yes, just like in Call the Midwife, the good old days as I reminisce now, watching the series on the telly.). She made all the plans for when I went into labour, and we had decided that a single bed would be put in the living room, in front of an open fire, and my husband could help all the way, including with the birth, and after the birth, our baby would be laid in a drawer, padded with blankets and laid in front of the fire, and my mother would take the other two little ones to her house when my labour started. Everything went to plan. I went into labour on the day that was predicted, my husband went to call the midwife from a phone box, Mum came around and took my two little girls, and hubby made sure there was lots of hot water at the ready. I knew the routine by now so stayed in my nightdress and just tried to relax and walk around the living room, stopping occasionally to hold on to a chair and do my breathing exercises like I had been told. Eventually, hubby came back and said that the midwife was on her way so I went to lay on the little single bed which was brought down from upstairs and put in front of the fire. The contractions were coming pretty regular now and I was very uncomfortable but didn't feel like pushing yet. My midwife arrived and got to work, making herself at home. The first thing she did was examine me and told me it wouldn't be long before I wanted to push so she got everything ready for the delivery and then asked my husband to put the kettle on and make a cuppa for the pair of them. Fuckin charming I thought to myself. They stood around drinking tea while I was rolling around the bed in agony now as the pains were bad and I eventually had the urge to push. Everything happened quickly after that. Hot water at the ready, husband holding me up, I was told to put chin on my chest and push with the next contraction. I pushed like my life depended on it, then as the pain subsided, I took a breather. The next contraction came and I pushed as hard as I could and kept doing that until the midwife said she could see the head and invited my husband to have a look. His face was a picture of amazement. 'Come on, Hazel, one last big push.'

And I did and out the baby popped. Thick dark hair, perfect little body of, (Yes, you've guessed it) another little girl. We could not have been happier. The midwife cut the cord, cleaned her up, and handed her to her dad.

My three daughters were all born in the 1960s. One after another, they came and it seemed like I was always pregnant and was happy with them being born so close together. I am addicted to the series "Call the Midwife" because that's how it was in my day. It may not have been in the east end of London, but it was just the same here in Nottingham. I was so proud of being pregnant all the time. The ante-natal clinics, the check-ups, and the feeling like I could go on being pregnant forever.

Pushing a pram with a baby in it, one sitting in a little chair on the front and one holding my hand. Watching that series brings back memories of my time, mine and my husband's, and it was a wonderful time, although I was a bastard later on. Every time I was pregnant, I was proud and happy and popped the babies out one after another. I vividly remember each birth but the one I remember the most was the birth of our third daughter, Trudy, who I had at home. It was the most wonderful feeling in the world. I remember my first love being there along with the midwife and demanded that he stay. It was just a single bed in front of an open coal fire, my husband and the midwife, who did turn up on a bike, just as in the series. I remember Stephen mixing the Dettol wrong, in fact, he was so nervous, he fucked up but he stayed close to me and I remember that when I was pushing, during my contractions, then panting when I was told, he had his arm under one of my legs and the midwife holding the other and my first husband looked between my legs and saw the head coming out of me and then the rest of my daughter being born. It felt so intimate and close. How can you put a price on that? I had a natural birth, as with the other two and we were both crying and emotional. There was no embarrassment, like in the early days of the TV Series when husbands were banned from the room. Husband and wife together, witnessing the birth of their baby. How close a bond can you get than that?

Now, my tears fall, yet again and I have to finish this chapter, although my heart will finally be broken in the future. Oh! How I hurt!

Chapter Three
Thoughts (Again)

Mum brought the two girls back to introduce them to their new baby sister and also delivered a big pot of stew as she thought I might be hungry. As I lay in bed, I held my new daughter to my breast and felt love like no other. I had my family around me, and three daughters, all in nappies at the same time. I had no idea how I was going to manage this. That was my first niggling thought but swiftly left me as I was drawn up into the moment of the present and this tiny little baby at my breast, family by my side and being in my own home. Life felt good at that moment. After my set amount of bed rest, as was the thing to do in those days, and visits from the midwife, things returned to normal. I went back to being a wife, mother, and lover.

Every day, I did the usual housewife stuff and it was really hard for me as I was still only a teenager myself. If I went to the shops, I had a baby in the pram, the middle one sitting on a small seat fixed across the front of the pram, and my oldest walking by my side, holding my hand. Also, these were the days of terry-towelling nappies, and I had washing lines full of them every day. We were happy but hubby still hadn't got a job and we were struggling and living on handouts from the family and for me, I was getting frustrated with just about everything. All I seemed to be doing was cooking, cleaning, and shopping, changing nappies again and again, and coping with three little girls. It was really hard for me and I was not getting help from anyone. By the time my new daughter was six months old, I realised that I had three children under the age of five and could not cope. Those thoughts again, coming into my head; where was my birth mother? God only knows after all this time but I kept thinking about her and the wandering restless gipsy in me began to surface again, and the thoughts that I wanted more than this. I was barely nineteen years old and my life had become boring, mundane, and frustrating. Life for me was at a standstill, but not for long, I do know that. One day, for whatever reason I do not know, I told my husband I was going out and just walked. I had a bit of money on me so I caught a bus to Nottingham to find that address that had been in my head seemingly forever. I found 85, Queens Drive where my birth mother was supposed to live, and knocked on the door, my heart racing. A strange lady opened the door and when I questioned her about a blonde-haired lady living there and why I was there, she told me the people who lived there before had long since left and gone to America. *Oh, shit*, I thought to myself. *Well, that's fucked my plans right up.* I said goodbye to the lady and something in my mind told me I didn't want to go home but to go across the road to the train station and get on a train to God knows where. In the sixties, you could buy platform tickets for tuppence from a machine. They were for people to be able to go onto the platform to meet friends and family. I bought one of those and went down onto a platform and just sat on a seat alone with my thoughts. I didn't want to go home to three crying babies, I wanted to find my real mother.

All I had were the clothes on my back, no money, and a platform ticket held tightly in my hand. I needed to keep moving so waited for the next train to come into the station and I would get on it and go wherever it took me. There were no ticket inspectors on the trains back then really so I reckon I could have a train ride for free. The next train that came in said London on the front, so I got on that. Didn't know where London was. I had never been outside Nottingham so it would just maybe take me closer to finding my real mum. I sat alone on that train and it was a long ride, which left me alone to think about what I was doing and what I had done. I had left three little girls, one only a baby, with my husband, no one had any idea where I was and I had nothing to my name.

Then guilt overtook me and I thought what a selfish, uncaring, negligent bastard of a mother I had turned out to be and I hated myself for that and do still to this day. I do know one thing though, I wanted to go to London, wherever that was, I wanted to stay on that train until the end of the line and just had to work out what story I was going to tell the guard at the end of the platform the other end as to why I hadn't got a ticket. Well, after what seemed like hours and me starting to get frightened, the train came to a halt in London. I jumped down off the train and looked around in amazement at how big the station was. Bloody hell, what have I let myself in for???

Now for the hardest part, trying to get the ticket collector to believe me. Walking up to him, I told him I had done wrong by not buying a ticket, but if I could give him my name and address in Nottingham, when I got back home later that day, I would get my mum to come to the station and bring some money with her to pay for my train fare. He asked me why I had come to London and I just bullshitted my way out of that by saying I just wanted to have a look at all the big shops and different places then I would go back home. He wrote out a form that passed as a ticket to get home and said he would phone Nottingham station to say that I would be returning later that day. He let me pass and I smiled. *Cracked it,* I thought to myself as I walked out of the station and into London, not having a bloody clue as to where I was going, how I was going to eat, or where I was going to sleep. Now I became concerned and guilty because of what I had done and wishing I hadn't but happy that I was in a place that felt exciting and busy and colourful. I just walked and walked, gazing at the huge buildings and the vast amount of people scurrying everywhere. I walked for hours and hours and came across a huge park called Hyde Park. Walking through that place, I sat on a park bench and counted what few pennies I had in my coat pocket. I needed a cup of tea and re-think my situation. I found a cafe nearby and sat in a corner by myself and felt a bit better with a warm drink inside me. I felt so lost. I wanted to go home then I didn't, then I did again. I realised what I had left behind and it was breaking me inside, but a part of me wanted to stay in London, wanting to find something but not knowing what. I felt so bloody sad and lost. It began to get dark and I decided that I would go back into the park and find somewhere to hide myself and sleep.

Bloody good job, it was summer and hot and dry, I thought to myself. In the end, I just ended up on a park bench and I was so tired I just curled my legs up under me and slept until morning. No one bothered me, there was no one around and I didn't really feel in any danger. It was just starting to get daylight as I woke up so I started to walk again. I ended up at a place called Piccadilly Circus. It was crowded with people and I really needed to pee, so, on looking around, I found that there was a train station with toilets. At least I could have a wash and make myself look a bit decent. Looking in a mirror in those toilets, my face looked tired but I was still pretty and young and when I walked the streets around Piccadilly Circus, I got looks from men, and I knew I looked sexy but that wasn't going to get me anywhere to stay and keep safe until I decided what I wanted to do. I wanted to go home but knew I had turned my back once again on my family who I loved dearly, I missed the turmoil I had, looking after my babies and knew that my husband really hated me for leaving like I had. Anyway, I was deep in my thoughts when a man approached me and asked if I would go with him and I could earn some money. Well, my ears pricked up at that and I tagged alongside him. He was nothing to look at and was a lot older than me. *Quite ugly as well*, I thought. He showed me a wad of money in his hand and led me to some stone basement stairs where, when we got to the bottom, he pushed me up against the wall and asked me to play with his dick and rub it until he came. I was terrified inside but did what he told me to and thought of the money.

I stared at the small wad of notes in my hand. *Oh well, that was easy,* I thought to myself! I looked at the one-pound note on top of the pile and decided to count it. I lifted up the pound note and just stood with my mouth open. All the rest of it was blank paper and all the same size as the one-pound note that was on top. I had been well and truly conned. *The bloody arsehole,* I thought to myself.

What a dirty trick to pull on me, but thinking back on it, I had been dirty myself and I felt ashamed of myself. By now, as I walked back up into the street, the ugly bastard had vanished into the crowd. Well, I was going to learn fast from now on but at least I had one pound and back in 1969, I sure could buy lots of cups of teas and maybe a sandwich. One pound went a long way in those days. Still with no plans, and the fact that it was getting dark, I made my way back to the park and found an empty bench and lay down with my legs tucked under me, and rested the best I could. No one bothered me, although there were some junkies around and dossers lying about, but I guess I looked like one of them so I was left alone. I did sleep, and when I woke up I did the same routine, going to the toilets in Piccadilly Circus underground station where I washed myself, and I even washed my panties and put them back on wet but at least I felt clean. Well, this routine carried on for about a week and one day after walking to find yet another cafe for yet another cup of tea, and my pound was dwindling by each cup of tea I drank, I found a little cheap one in Soho, apparently in the heart of London's west end. Putting myself in a corner out of the way, I was trying my best to make my cuppa last as long as possible, and I needed a much-longed-for rest anyway. Sitting there, deep with my own thoughts, a man came and sat next to me. He was well dressed, black suit and tie but I thought to myself, *Oh no! I'm not falling for any of that shit again.* He was very pleasant and asked me what I was up to. I told him I had nowhere to live, and I needed to make some money. He introduced himself as Doug and told me he worked as a manager of the club next door. I hadn't even noticed a club anywhere. Then he asked me if I would like a job as a stripper. I just about choked on my tea.

'A what?'

I didn't even know what one of those was. He explained that girls go on a little stage, under lights, and while they are dancing to music, they start taking their clothes off until they are naked while men sitting in front of the stage just watch them, then when you are naked, you pose as the curtains close. What the bloody hell was life going to throw at me next, I wondered. He told me that if I was any good, his boss would keep me on permanently and I would be earning a wage of sixteen pounds and ten shillings a week. Christ, that sounded like a lot of money to me at that moment so I agreed to try. I told him that I had never done this sort of thing before so I might not be any good.

'I will be the judge of that,' and with that said, he told me to wait in the cafe while he went up the road to buy me something sexy to wear on stage. *Well!* I thought to myself, I think I might have landed on my feet here, so just sat and waited for Doug to come back.

Well, he returned about ten minutes later with a bag full of clothes, and asked me to follow him next door, where he continued to take me up the stairs to a dressing room full of semi-naked or naked young girls. Doug told me to get dressed in the clothes he bought and keep my high heels on at the end. The bag contained a black negligee, a bra and a G-string, which tied at the sides so it came off more easily. Oh! And a feather boa. What the hell was I supposed to do with that? Oh! I know, waft it about when I was eventually naked. Oh, Christ, I was so very scared. I was going to dance for ten minutes to the theme music from the film *The Good, The Bad and The Ugly.*

'Okay,' said Doug, 'you are on. Go down those stairs and stand on stage behind the curtains and when the music starts, the curtains will open and you start dancing as sexy as you can.'

Bloody Nora, I thought to myself. I have only ever been sexy with my husband, now I have to do it in front of an audience full of men who would be waiting to see my body. I really had nothing to show. I was skinny, with thin legs and tiny boobs. Who in their right minds would get a thrill out of that I wondered, but I needn't have worried because all the men did. I tried to be as sexy as possible but could feel my knees knocking. Well, I did the best I could and when the music finished, as the curtains closed, the men were applauding like mad. I climbed those stairs feeling elated and was met by Doug who actually said that with practice I could become a good stripper. *Wow!* I thought, that felt good to hear and I would be earning a wage every week as well. Doug then turned to me and said very quietly to me that I could live with him until I got settled and that I would be safe. I stayed in the dressing room all day after that and went on stage once every two hours until midnight when the club closed.

The manager offered to let me stay with him at his house outside London, I looked at him fearfully, wondering if I was going to get ripped off again, or maybe hurt, but he promised that I could stay with him and he would not touch me. He seemed kind and very effeminate and dainty in his demeanour so I said yes, I would stay with him. He locked up the club and I waited at the door while he went and fetched his car. Bloody hell, there he was pulling up in a big PINK! Cadillac. I could not believe it. *There is no turning back now, Hazel,* I thought to myself. I knew I was going to do well here, and as they say, "Practice makes perfect," and boy! Was I going to practice! Every day he took me to work, and NO! Nothing did happen in bed. He never made a move on me. I enjoyed working at this club. It was called the "Playboy Club" on Wardour Street in Soho and was well known. Doug helped me choose outfits and make-up and proper dance shoes and my acts got better and sexier. I would say it was a cross between striptease and burlesque. In the late '60s, pole dancing and lap dancing hadn't been invented. It was stage work only so you never got touched by the men and you had to really work hard at being a tease in front of them, hence the word striptease.

My stripping days

I began to love it. I enjoyed showing off my body and I enjoyed the men seeing my nakedness and get a thrill out of it. One day, Doug came to me and asked if I would like to work in another club as well. At least it would double my money. I jumped at the chance and he took me to a club called Maxim's. It was run by a man who was the owner and he was Jewish and his name was Murray. I was doing good in my work by then so he found a costume in the dressing room for me and said to me, 'Well let's see what you can do.'

My stripping days

My costume consisted of a bra, suspenders and stockings, a red, see-through mini dress and a big floppy hat and I went onto a big oval stage and I danced to "The Stripper" by David Rose followed by "The Girl" from Ipanema. Apart from not knowing that there really was a special way to take stockings off when you danced, I thought I did really well and felt good when the men applauded me. I really was getting the hang of things more now and the more I danced, the braver I became when I was naked. I strutted my stuff up and down the stage, back straight, legs open, and always making eye contact with the men like they were the only ones that mattered. I learned how to pout properly (yes, there is a proper way to make a pout with your lips). I learned how to work on the floor, naked and getting in such positions as to give the men watching me just a little glimpse of my pussy and just as quickly, take it away from them. Part of one of my acts was working with my back to the men, and as I contorted my body, every part of me was on view, full throttle. The audience loved it and I became popular, very popular. I began to remember the streets, watched other girls work, and found that a girl would work four or five clubs, every two hours, then do them all over again and you would work twelve hours a day. From 12 noon until midnight. It looked exhausting and it was, but in time, I did it and eventually worked five clubs, running from one to another every two hours then doing it all over again. With the money I was earning, I could afford to buy my own dancing clothes for each different act in each different club. Doug asked me if I wanted just one more club called the Dolls House at the top of Dean Street in the middle of Soho. All the clubs were very close together and there were a lot of them. I jumped at the chance of this and found out that this club was owned by a French man and had a dance teacher named Rhoda Rogers who I later found out was in the variety business and very famous in Europe and England. She was a business-woman and a very good dance teacher and I had to go for an interview with her to see if I was good enough. It was very posh compared to the others so I went on the stage, which was round and small, and with the music they had given me, I danced my best. Rhoda and a male stripper were out front watching me and when I had finished, I went upstairs and waited to see if had been accepted. Rhoda came up and told me she would give me a trial run and told me to be in for ten o'clock the next morning for rehearsals. Well, bugger me, I'm in hopefully but just did not realise how hard the work would be because Rhoda wanted nothing but perfection on stage from her girls. She taught me how to take off my stockings sexily, and believe me it's harder than you think, but I got the hang of it. She showed me how to work with a chair, under it, over it and sitting on it backwards and forwards. It was so hard doing that and all the while taking an item of clothing off as well. I learned how to take off items of clothing with my teeth. Rhoda was quite pleased with my actions and was prepared to give me a job, and I was about to enter a very dangerous part of my life but didn't know it yet. (God help me.)

The Playboy Club

Chapter Four
Danger Lurks

I had got to know all the streets quite well now in Soho, as they were all pretty close together. One day, as I walked backed to the Playboy club, I noticed a man looking at me and smiling. He was very handsome, much older than me and not English. I walked past him every two hours, and still, he smiled at me, finally calling me over. I went, like a lamb to the slaughter because he was so good looking and smartly dressed.

'I've been watching you going to and fro to your clubs. Would you be interested if I got you some work in a couple more?'

I nodded my head and said, 'Yes okay,' and before I knew it, he had pushed me up against the doorway and kissed me. Telling me he was Maltese and was working on a door of what was known as a Clip Joint, that is where he calls men in off the street and he talks them into going to a strip club if they pay him a fee, then when he gets them to a strip club, they have to pay again. He worked on commission, he told me, and he could get me into a couple of clubs that were run by his boss. I agreed and told him I would come and see him when I had finished my act at the Playboy Club on Wardour Street. With that, he let me go and said he would wait for me. Couldn't wait, really as he was quite a dish and I liked him.

Got on with my act at the club, then got dressed and rushed back around the corner to see if he was still there. Yep, he was waiting for me and we sat talking for a while. He asked where I came from, asked me where I was living and asked if I would like to go and live with him. Well, that took me by surprise but when he told me he lived by himself, I thought to myself, '*Why not?*' It's not as if I'm in a relationship with Dougie because he treated me more like a sister than a girlfriend. I said yes and with that, he took me to a club called The Red Mill which was just around the corner from the Playboy. He spoke to the big boss in a language I didn't understand, later finding out that it was Maltese and he said he would give me a spot in his show. Little did I know that this big boss was one of the two men who ran the Maltese Mafia at that time. I met them both eventually, the first one who gave me a job was named Frank Mifsud, and the other one I later found out was Bernie Silver and I got to know that they ran most of the strip clubs, and prostitute hovels in Soho. It was all still new to me and I really was still very innocent, only working for three English clubs up until now. I was to start the next day, and I was okay with that. Then he took me to another club run by the Maltese named The Carnival Club on Old Compton Street and got me a ten-minute slot there. By now, I had five clubs on the go, just like all the other girls, and found myself just running from one to another with hardly any time in between to eat and keep my energy up.

One of the girls offered me a blue pill. She told me it would give me lots more energy and I wouldn't feel like eating. I found out later that they were amphetamines or speed, never heard of them either but I felt great once it started working and raced 'round the clubs, feeling full of energy. *Bloody great*, I thought and would ask for another one the next day. In the meantime, I broke my news to Dougie in the playboy club that I would be leaving that night and going home with a man who had become my friend and staying with him. He warned me to be very careful and that he would always be there for me if I wanted to come back. With that, I carried on working really hard and by the time midnight came and I had done my last act, there he was, my new Maltese boyfriend, waiting to take me home. I was a little bit nervous but I think he could see that in my face and told me not to worry. He drove his car and parked in front of a big old house, but he led me down into the dingy basement and unlocked a door to a basement room. *This was where he lived,* I thought. *Fuck me, what have I got myself into.* Frank told me he was going to run me a bath, and even that was shared by other people in this big old house. I had my bath and went back to the room where I was going to stay with him. In my head, I couldn't resist him. He was so handsome and sweet-talking.

We got into bed and he started kissing me and lay on top of me and started to make love to me. I told him not to come inside me as I had no protection from getting pregnant. I don't think he thought of my feelings at all because, after a minute, it was over. He ejaculated over my stomach and fell straight to sleep. Crikey! *Was that it?* I questioned myself. To be honest, I felt nothing at all but fell asleep in his arms anyway because I liked the man. I'm afraid that's how it was going to be every time we got in bed. And still, I stayed. I was so knackered when I eventually woke the next morning as it had taken me ages to fall asleep because that little blue speed pill was in my system.

We drove into Soho at about 10 am the next morning and he took me to a hairdresser to get my hair done, then to a shop where I could sit in a chair and have hot towels put on my face for a few minutes to cleanse my skin as Frank had said. It felt really weird but hey! I wasn't complaining because my face felt fresh and as I made my way to my first club, The Playboy, to put on my make-up and get ready for my act, Frank said he would meet me in my break. *I never get a bleeding break,* I thought to myself and went to see if I could find a girl who had another one of those little blue pills to keep me going. Seemed easy in the late '60s because they were everywhere. I took one and within five minutes, it started to work and I felt elated and full of energy. Full make-up, hair done, ready for the busy day, I went to work. I did manage to see my new boyfriend in one of my breaks and he took me for something to eat. It was breakfast. Although it looked delicious, every mouthful kept going 'round and 'round in my mouth and I was finding it hard to swallow any of it. I picked out the softest food and ate then said I had to go to my next club. My man from Malta never suspected anything so I got away with that. Well, life carried on the same after that, go on stage, take my clothes off seductively, finish naked, run upstairs to the dressing room, get my street clothes back on and run to my next club. In the end, I was working five clubs and earning a lot of money, only I wasn't, and why? I hear you say. Well, the smooth-talking boyfriend was waiting outside each club on a Saturday night and asked me to hand over my wage packet, that he would keep my money safe and, in a few weeks, we could probably get another flat, a posher one instead of the flea pit we were living in now. I never thought anything about it and handed over my wage packets, but one thing puzzled me, he never gave me any money back for myself. He began to buy my clothes for me, my make-up, he would order my food in restaurants, cook when we got home, but still never clocked on that I was taking speed pills to keep me going. I barely touched any food and lived on pills to keep me going, the only side effect being that I couldn't sleep when we got home as I was wired. I started to lose weight and he couldn't understand that until one day I was in the dressing room of the Playboy club, and knew I had half a tablet in the bottom of my always empty purse. As I opened my purse, he came racing into the dressing room, grabbed my purse from me and found my half pill and just before I was ready to go on stage, and in front of all the other girls, he smacked me so hard across my face, I thought my head was going to fall off. He took my purse, stormed off, and told me never to take any more. Everyone just stood there keeping quiet and it seemed that they were used to seeing boyfriends of the girls, coming in and hitting them or shouting at them. Seemed to me it was run of the mill.

I went on stage with my face bloody hurting, but after my act, I went to see him and told him I was sorry and that I wouldn't do it again. 'I hate drugs,' he said to me through gritted teeth but accepted that I was truly sorry.

Well, I worked hard and couldn't sleep because of the speed racing around my body, but did know that I would try and get some more, even behind his back. Trouble was, I never had any money to buy them because he never gave me any money, not even for a cuppa. I had to ask him for everything. One night, in the middle of the night, I was trying to sleep and he was asleep when there was a knock at the door. He got up to answer and a middle-aged woman was standing there. I sat up, quite shocked because there I was, sitting up in bed, naked, with a sheet covering me. Frank introduced her as Gina, his wife from Malta. I sat there absolutely fucking stupefied. I didn't know what to do or say, and they were talking in a different language.

The prick never told me he was married. Oh, *Christ! What have I got myself into now?* Seeing as it was nearly morning, I went to have a bath and get ready for work and his wife started asking me questions as she spoke quite good English. 'How long you been here with him then? I stammered a bit and told her quite a few months.

That's why he's been sending me money for me and the kids in Malta then. It finally sunk in, so that's why he wanted my wages every week then, what a bastard, and I had been and was still under his spell. I dare not say anything so just carried on getting ready. Well I thought, this is a weird situation to find myself in, but had to go with the flow because I knew if I started moaning about her being there, I would get a smack in the mouth or worse. I think they call it grooming these days and thinking back to the very first time I met him and how suave he was, and how he managed to coax me into the palm of his hand then because I was young, that's what he was doing with me too.

Well, we all arrived in Soho together, the three of us and he sent us both to the hairdressers together and we sat next together and we both got hair extensions in our hair and we both looked good. I hated when we were together and the bastard and his wife started talking to each other in their own language, Maltese.

I also hated when I was working, thinking what they were getting up to. Still, I kept going and halfway through the day, Sir took me to one side and said she would be staying with us the night before she went back to Malta to their two sons and we would be sharing the same bed that night and wouldn't it be fun if us ladies both got a bit drunk and had sex together while he watched. *You've got to be kidding me,* I thought. I' had never done anything with a woman before but just nodded like the dumb prat I was. Night time drew in and midnight was getting closer and I could tell just by looking at the wife's face, she was looking jittery as well. Well, we both had a bath and then sat together in bed, not knowing what to do, honestly, we really didn't.

'Well, get on with it then.'

'What!' We both said at the same time.

'Well, start kissing and stroking each other, I promise I won't touch either of you. I just want to watch.'

Well, we started doing just that but about halfway through, as we both didn't drink and were not used to whisky, we both puked down either side of the bed. I had never drunk alcohol before and she must have but didn't like it so seeing us both puking put paid to that little experiment and to top it all off, he slept on the end of the bed next to HER! I just wanted to sleep and quickly get to work the next day, just to get away from both of them.

Well, what a special day the next day was going to bring at the Playboy Club. When I arrived, I was told that the television people were making a documentary about Wardour Street and that the Playboy Club was going to be included and would I like to be filmed doing my act on stage. It was going to be a half-hour programme and would be advertised in the TV Times magazine with a two-page spread about me in the middle. 'Oh Boy! Yes, please. How exciting.'

It was the early seventies when colour television had not long happened and I was going to be on TV. The programme was going to be called "Celluloid Village of Dreams" and would be about life on Wardour Street, one of the main parts of London to do with the film industry. I stuck to my guns when I told the Maltese prick what I was doing. It wouldn't take me away from my other clubs and would not take long. As I had already said yes, there was nothing he could do and I also never said goodbye to Gina either. To be honest, I was glad to see her go but had wised up to what he was up to even though I carried on giving him my wage packets every week. Basically, he was a sort of pimp, wasn't he?

But stripping instead of prostituting myself. Must admit though, he was always in the background somewhere.

That day was brilliant. A man came into the dressing room with a cameraman to do the interview which was to be put into the TV Times magazine. He asked me about my life and my job and I had photos taken. Also, they televised me walking into the club from the street. The cameras then moved into the auditorium and placed themselves amongst the punters and filmed small parts of the act I did on stage. I felt so proud of myself for doing that and it was televised on what then used to be called A.T.V. Many years later, I asked ATV if they could find that programme in their archives.

After a couple of weeks, I received a copy of it on DVD for my memory box and I also still have a copy of the TV Times magazine. How cool is that! Anyway back to my story, life went on as normal, and yes, I was still with the ratbag and yes, I was still handing over my money but I was also well dressed, looked good, and was a bloody good stripper. He took care of me, the big mafia bosses took care of their girls and big Frank Mifsud who was around most of the time, was always pleasant to me, smoked cigars and you would not cross the man, trust me. I imagine those two men were as bad as the Krays. I did find out in later years though that the Krays did try and take over the Soho Scene.

They didn't have much luck though and kept to the east end. Life carried on as normal for me. As we were now into the 1970s, the acts in some of the clubs got more raunchy, and at the carnival club, I did an act on stage with another girl and it was a schoolgirl act, which meant we had to dress up in school uniforms and slowly but innocently, get down to the nitty-gritty of pretending to make lesbian love on stage and end up naked before the end. Well, that did go down a treat with the audience but I think we went a bit over the top, according to the rules, we made it look too real and got too intimate and after working that number for a few days, it was taken out of the show. 'Damn it, it was a bloody good act as well.' This happened at the Carnival Club, one which was run by the Maltese Mafia and I think that, as the police came to visit the manager every Saturday night for a pay-off so that whatever happened on stage, could stay on stage, but after watching my act with the other girl, I think they had a strong word, and that was why we were told it had to go. Oh well! It was nice while it lasted. Another act that I did on stage, at the Dolls House at the top of Dean Street, the club run by the beautiful Rhoda Rogers, took a lot of rehearsing and a lot of different lighting to make it work. It included a fully size dummy of a man who would have an artificial cock strapped to him (dildo) and would be laid on a table full length of the stage, behind a flimsy curtain, and to begin with, I had to work the front of the stage, slowly ending up naked, then as the curtains parted, revealing this "MAN" lying on the table with a bloody great hard-on, and I had to climb on to him, sideways on to the stage and the men, and I had to have sex with him or make it look like I did. Now the secret was in the lighting overhead. As I moved, the lighting moved so it was never pointed between my legs, so the secret being, was I actually sitting on the dildo or wasn't I? It was difficult for me to sit on that thing and pretend to be sensual, without it going up inside me. I must admit that sometimes it did start to enter me but mostly I managed to sit on it whilst it was flat on his body. 'Thank God for good stage lighting.'

It was really amusing to watch the men in the audience, first they strained their necks one way, then the lighting changed and they strained their necks the other way, not quite sure whether that dildo was inside me or not, but it never was, but the punters didn't know that. I often think just how many men in that auditorium were masturbating while they watched me. It looked so real and I had to pretend to have an orgasm at the end. What an act that was and Rhoda kept that one in the show for about three months. The punters would be waiting outside the club just before the doors opened at 12 noon, just so that they could get a good front-row seat. I must admit, I enjoyed doing that act immensely although I had to work really hard whilst sitting on that dummy with a dildo, that it never went inside me as that would be considered immoral and could get the club in a whole lot of trouble.

Thank God for a good stage lighting manager because one light in the wrong place at that time could have ruined it all. I was loving my work, and doing so many different acts in different clubs. The pimp and I had moved to a nice bedsit in Islington and life carried on as normal. I was a really good stripper and burlesque dancer now and a lot of places wanted to have me in their shows, which was good because I was getting a name for myself.

It was one morning while I was getting ready for work that there was a knock on our door. Frank went to answer it, turned to me, and said someone wanted to speak to me. I stood at the door unable to speak. There in front of me stood my sister, the one who I fleetingly saw when I was sixteen, holding my first baby, and a young teenage lad standing next to her who she introduced as my brother Danny. I knew nothing of him at all, but apparently had two of them. Danny and Jimmy. I invited them in and she told me that they had been searching for me for a long time and that they still lived in Alicante in Spain and that my birth mother wanted to see me and go and live with them. Well, I was dumbfounded because after all that I had gone through in the past, because I had tried to find her and because of the fact that if it wasn't for her, I would not have walked away from my husband and children, I didn't know what to say. I asked them to come with me to work and they agreed as they wanted to talk more with me. Frank looked at me and just shrugged his shoulders as if he didn't give a shit. In fact, he had been getting bored with me for some time and even though I was still giving him my wage packets, and I was still getting the odd slap for no reason, I stuck with him. I had been totally groomed by now but was getting a bit pissed off with him. I think the novelty was wearing a bit thin now and I certainly didn't love him one little bit. I also think he was cheating on me and I also think he would not have any problem getting some girl to replace me to make money for him. My sister told me that they would be leaving at the weekend, so would Frank let me go. I spoke to him in one of my breaks between shows and asked if I could go? He told me he had no problem with it and I could pack everything by the end of the week. *I bet he's got someone else to take my place already,* I thought to myself. What a rotten shitbag he was and I was hating him more and more.

Frank brought me a big trunk to pack all my stuff into, and my sister had bought me a one-way ticket to Alicante for the week after so that gave me time to hand in my notice in all my clubs and get ready. I was excited and after all these years of looking for my real mother, I was finally going to meet her. Frank made sure he packed everything and he also made sure that he collected my wage packets from me on Saturday night too and told me I would fly out the next day. What a heartless bastard he was, leaving me without any money. All this happened the following week, so I got Frank to phone my sister and tell her the day I would be arriving and to meet me. Well, the day arrived and with my trunk packed up in the back of his car, my thieving bloody boyfriend left me at Heathrow airport to find my own way to get to the plane. As he turned to go, I thought to myself, *good riddance you bastard, now I will be able to have a good rest away from you, you arsehole.*

Well, the flight didn't last long but as I had no money, I was unable to buy a drink or anything to eat. Still, it didn't take long to get there and when I climbed down the steps of the plane and onto the runway, there was my sister and two brothers to meet me, one of whom I had never met. My trunk was unloaded and Jimmy, the youngest brother dragged it to the car park, loaded it and then we were on our way to where they all lived in a little part of Alicante called Alburfereta. Parking up outside this house was amazing. It was a villa of sorts and was right on the sea. The weather was hot and the villa was beautiful. Sandra, my sister took me to the bedroom I would be sharing with her and I settled in. My brothers were handsome-looking lads and my sister had blonde hair right down to her bum. It was so hot and as I stood on the balcony overlooking the sea, I said I was going to put a swimsuit on and go in the water. No one was worried and so off I went. I was told later that my mother and father were at the air force base and would be home tomorrow. I was okay with that and looked forward to meeting them. As the day went on, my two brothers suggested they would take me to look around where I was going to live. Well, I was taken to a nightclub, (never been in one of those before) and my two new brothers were wild and crazy and we all drank alcohol (me for the second time) and we ate Spanish sausage and after that, I can barely remember getting back to my new home but do remember being violently sick outside the door. I was put to bed and surfaced the next day feeling like absolute bloody rubbish. Slowly coming around, I remembered that my real mum was coming home today to see me so I hung around more with my two brothers than I did with my sister. She seemed a bit uppity and la de la, as if she was too good and better than me, but then again, she did have a job and could speak fluent Spanish, so I suppose she was. As the day wore on, all of a sudden, as I sat in the living room, I heard footsteps and the unmistakable voice of a woman saying, 'Oh where's my baby, where is my daughter?' Then there she stood in the doorway.

I was hugged and kissed and was surprised to notice that she looked like an older version of me. Blonde hair, blue eyes, well dressed, and loads of make-up on. This was the first time I had met her properly and now I could really find out more about her. Said hello to my dad, who wasn't really. I had a different dad and my mother never told me who he was. In fact, all of us had different fathers. *Christ*, I thought, she put it about a bit but kept my thoughts to myself. Well, the days turned into months and months. I hadn't got a job as I didn't speak Spanish and just lounged around on the patio all day getting a lovely tan. Sandra, my sister went to work every day, I stayed lounging around in the sun in my bikini, every so often, my brothers took me on the back of their motocross bikes, tearing around the hills and speeding so I clung for dear life, usually on the back of Jimmy's bike. It was hair raising and I loved it. One day, we arrived back at the villa to hear Mum and Dad screaming, in the middle of one big argument in the kitchen. Would you believe it was about me? Mum had been drinking a bit and was screaming at her husband that he fancied me because she used to look like me when she was younger and when I went in, she told me to leave, to fuck off and not live there anymore.

Chapter Five
Fury!

As mothers go, she seemed to be acting like the mother from hell right now. Why was she acting like this? She accused her husband, who was not my father and not even my step-father. She had accused him of coming on to me when I knew that he hadn't. He always looked at me, especially when I was walking around in a bikini because it was always hot. Well, that wasn't unusual, I had always walked around half-naked for a few years because of my job in London and I did not think I was doing anything wrong. If she had noticed him watching me all the time, then it was his problem, not mine and they were fighting like hell in the kitchen and I had just walked into World War III.

After he had told her to shut up, she turned to me and with evil fire in her eyes had told me I was not wanted there and to 'fuck off' simple as that. Well, my temper had started to get the better of me now and I screamed at her that I had no money to get back to England and nowhere to go here in Spain. 'I don't give a shit,' she yelled, 'just get out of here and don't come back.'

I was shaking with anger and crying at the same time and I noticed that my two brothers and my sister just stood there watching, not saying a word. I don't know why they were so quiet, they had no reason to get involved. My sister had a dad who she didn't know, I had a different dad who I never did and never would know and Jimmy, the youngest brother had a father that my mum had an affair with whilst travelling on a cargo ship with her husband. I think Danny was the only one that came from the man she was now screaming at, and as far as I was concerned, I hated her and to me, she was nothing but a whore. I ran out of the side door of the villa, down the steep rocks near the sea, taking nothing with me. No money and not one single item of clothing except the shorts that I had on and a little t- shirt and sandals. I ran across the road to a little outside bar and just sat at a table crying like hell.

The barman must have felt sorry for me when I tried to explain what had just happened and put a glass of wine in front of me and I just sat there for the longest time, not knowing what had just happened to turn my life upside down but gathered that my bitch of a birth mother did not want me at all. I hated her with a bloody vengeance then but more worrying was the fact that I was now homeless again, vowing never to set foot in that villa again. Well, I sat and I sat and no family came to find me and I think as it began to get dark, and although the bar was full of laughing happy people, the barman, in broken English, asked if I wanted somewhere to stay that night out of harm's way. I just looked at him, reminding myself in my head that I had come across a lot of men in my time in London, promising me the world and it had all turned to shit so I eyed him suspiciously.

'Don't worry,' he said with a smile. 'I live with my boyfriend and you will be safe. You can stay until you sort yourself out.'

Thank God for that, I thought, at least I won't get molested by two blokes who sleep together so I said yes. 'Okay. Thanks very much.'

After closing the bar that night, I went with him to where they both lived. It was just along the road from where my nightmare mother was but I didn't care as I never wanted to see her again. He introduced me to his boyfriend Phillipe, and I found out the other one's name was Marco. I was treated with kindness and they must have felt sorry for me because they told me I could stay with them as long as I liked and even gave me a bit of Spanish money to carry about with me. Days turned into weeks and I really didn't know what was going to happen to me. My friend, the barman made sure I had food and drink, and I hung around the bar all day, the bar, only being a little shack with a few tables outside was perfect and I felt safe there. I put on weight and had a lovely tan and no one bothered me at all. Another shock was waiting for me on the horizon pretty soon though, and it was a shock I was not expecting at all. I was sitting at a table alone one night around 5 pm and walking towards me was the gangster from London with my sister. Nearly falling off my stool, I got up and tried to kick the shit out of her, but Frank, yes, "the bloody gangster" stopped me and sat next to me.

I did not know why he was there until my sister told me my bastard mother had phoned him and told him to come and take me home. Sandra told us that she had booked a hotel for the night for us in Alicante city and my shit of a mother had bought two single tickets back to London in a couple of days. I was really happy to be getting away from there, to be honest but I would miss the sun and sea. I asked Marco if he would go and fetch my trunk full of clothes from the villa which was only across the road from the bar and drag it to his apartment. Told Frank to stay where he was and we would go out later for a meal but I needed to get my clothes from my friend's flat. Popping over to the boys' place, I found out that they had already got the trunk from my mother's and dragged it to their apartment. I wanted to change my clothes, so opened the trunk, and started rummaging through my clothes. Hang on a minute? As I picked up each item of clothing, I discovered that every single item of my clothes had been cut into shreds. I had day wear, evening gowns. In that trunk, there was everything I owned and every item had been sliced to shreds and destroyed. Every single item and been cut so bad that they could never be worn. I was told later that it was my mother and my youngest brother Jimmy who had done that. What an evil little shit my brother turned out to be, but found out later in life that he was a mummy's boy and her favourite and would do anything for her, including cutting up my clothes. Boy! Did I hate him! In fact, I hated every one of them and thought back to everything I had gone through in my past to get here to see my birth mother and I was absolutely furious with all of them. They were selfish people and never thought of anyone but themselves. *Bollocks to them,* I thought to myself, *I will gladly go back to England just to get away from these poison filled people.*

Then, the embarrassing fact that I had to go back to the bar, and tell Frank what had happened to all my clothes. He was angry, but not at me. As luck would have it, my snooty sister had given him the reservation slip for the hotel in Alicante which was already paid for, and I knew a little restaurant just down the road where we could eat. Luckily, he had some money on him. It was Pesetas in those days because euros hadn't been invented. Off we went as it started to get dark. The meal was nice. I had fish, he had steak but it was not long after that, he started to feel unwell and started to be violently sick. I asked a waiter if he could call a taxi to take us into Alicante to our hotel, which he did. As we waited outside, standing side by side, BANG! Straight into my face. The twat had swiped me so hard in the face for no reason except that it was my fault for giving him food poisoning. Well, well, well, he hadn't fucking changed, had he and knew I would have a right shiny black eye in the morning. Well, there was one thing he was, same old, same old.

Back at the hotel, we had single beds and frank just crawled into his, groaning all night. *Serves you right, you prick. Why didn't you just stay in London where you belong?* I thought to myself. The next morning, looking in the mirror, I had the black eye, just like I predicted, and twat face was feeling better and came over and told me to come back to bed. I knew what was coming and I thought, *Oh God, do I have to?*

Well, Hazel, I thought to myself, *look at the ceiling and think of England,* which I did and it was soon over, which didn't surprise me. He took me out and bought me a load of new clothes though, so I changed and then we made our way to the airport. No one from the family came to see us and if they had, I would have knocked the shit out of them all, especially my mother, who I hated with a vengeance. Good job, no one turned up.

Well, the flight was uneventful and Frank's car was parked in the car park. Now, the mini car had turned into an XJ6 Jaguar, bright red. Crikey, he must have done well for himself while I've been away, thinking to myself that he must have come for me because he has no one in his life right now and needed to put me back to work. We also had a new home, a flat in Maida Vale which was quite posh. I had the few clothes I had bought back from Spain, but Frank bought me a few more so I could get started again in the clubs who, when they all saw the different me, fattened out to perfection and healthily tanned, had no problem in giving me my jobs back. *Well, babe,* I thought to myself, *here we go again.* I still stuck with him, although he had treated me bad in the past. He looked after me well and I worked hard but he still waited outside each club ready to collect my wage packets. This went on for ages and it must have been 1974/75. I was soon getting bored again and back on the speed pills without him knowing.

One night walking down Dean Street coming from the Dolls House Club, I passed a little alleyway, which turned out to be the back door to a Hungarian Restaurant, and there stood a boy, younger than me, with chef's whites on, having a break from work and smiling at me as I walked past him. This went on for a few nights and he finally plucked up the courage to ask my name and told me he fancied me. I was really flattered and I sneaked into the passageway and we kissed. He was handsome and I was putty in his hands and do you know something, I didn't feel guilty one little bit about the so-called pimp I was living with, although every time we took the chance to kiss, I had to keep looking over my shoulder just in case I got caught. I told him all my problems, told him about my boyfriend and how nasty he could be and I was getting fed up with him. He told me that he would try and sort something out for me but it may take a while. We kissed and he told me to be patient. I was happy to wait, knowing I would get away from Frank's clutches as I was still getting grief from him, still got the odd smack in the face. In my breaks between clubs, which didn't last long I might add, I sat with my pimp on some steps near Ronnie Scott's jazz club on Frith Street and I just about had time to have a cuppa and a sandwich. I didn't eat much because the amphetamine pills I was taking, dulled my appetite and the food just kept going 'round and 'round in my mouth for what seemed like forever. Anyway, it was time for me to go and I left, saying I would be back in my next break, and walked around the corner onto Old Compton Street. On the corner, there was an amusement arcade called the golden goose. There were slot machines and one-armed bandits in there, kids used to go in there all the time. From out of nowhere, a car pulled up and two or maybe three men jumped out of the car and ran into the arcade. Suddenly, some shots rang out and everyone on the street froze in terror. The men jumped back in the car and drove off at speed. It was over in seconds and before anything else happened, most people just ran screaming or, as far as I was concerned, I just kept bloody walking trying to be normal. I ignored everyone around me and just went on with my day like most of the girls did. As I walked back to Frith Street to meet up with Frank, before I went to the Carnival Club, I noticed that most of Old Compton Street was cordoned off but I managed to get onto Frith Street for my break.

'What happened?' I asked.

He turned to me and in a whisper told me that Italian Tony had been shot to death in the arcade. Bloody hell, I was in shock. I knew his girlfriend who was a stripper like me and couldn't believe that he was dead. He was a nice bloke who I spoke to regularly, ate in the same Maltese restaurant on Frith Street which was up some narrow stairs off the street there, and just knew him as Tony. I knew he was a gangster, but most of the Maltese who hung around on Frith Street were also gangsters and the girls quickly learned to keep quiet about anything they saw and I mean anything. I later learned that it may have been a murder of revenge but never really found out except that it was a contract killing. He had been a naughty boy and when you are naughty and, in the Mafia, you more than likely end up dead like him. That's why the girls went about their work and saw nothing and said nothing because all of us knew what would happen if we did. That was how the Maltese Mafia worked and that's how the girls worked and lots of times, you saw at least one or the other girls come to work with a black eye or bruise somewhere on their body, but no one ever questioned it as it seemed to be acceptable because most of the strippers were controlled by Maltese boyfriends. I met many famous people in Soho which became natural. I stood behind Roger Moore as he was buying steak, I passed Danny La Rue in his day clothes going to his show, I even saw Ken Loach having a drink in the Venus rooms on Old Compton Street as I was working there. I also bumped into Christopher Lee coming out of the Gargoyle Drinking Club as I was on my way to yet another club called the Paradise Strip Club. Anyway, enough of that side of my life which I rarely speak of nowadays. I carried on having quick snuggles with the Hungarian chef and he told me one day if I wanted to get away from my gangster boyfriend, I could always stay with him but he lived in a bedsit in a large house, run by a very strict woman whose rules were "NO GIRLS". He let me know what time he finished work and lived in a house on Russell Square, just a little away from the west end. We arranged to meet up the next night and I agreed to be at the place he told me to be. This was it then. The great escape. I knew I had to get away for good this time. Had to get away from the violence, the slaps I was getting on a regular basis for no reason, to keep me in line, I suppose, and things I was witnessing on a weekly basis. Things were looking up hopefully.

Now, all I had to do was find a way of vanishing from Soho, even if it was in the middle of the day. The next morning, I got ready for work as normal but also knew that I could not take any clothes with me because that would arise suspicion. I did manage though, amongst some of my costumes, to put a few pairs of panties in my bag. I packed in my make-up, climbed into my bell-bottom jeans, a little top, and a short leather jacket. That was it. I was done. My stomach was churning but I had a plan and hoped it would work. I began my days' work in the clubs, going from one to the other, finally walking towards Broadwick Street. As Frank the pimp was nowhere to be seen when approaching the Paradise club, I knew this was it, I had to do this one thing. I had to keep walking straight past the club into the unknown yet again, but at least if I could get away from Soho for now and meet up later with my handsome toyboy cook who had offered me a roof over my head until we had decided what to do and all I knew was that he had to sneak me in very quietly to his room because of the landlady and her rule of "NO WOMEN". Well, here goes! I walked towards the Paradise Club but instead of turning in, I just kept walking on and on, too scared to look behind me, but the doorman didn't notice me anyway as he was talking to a customer. On and on I kept walking, with no idea where I was going. I knew that I had to get as far away as I could from the Soho streets because once word had got back to Frank that I hadn't turned up for my act, he would be looking for me. I just carried on walking, absolutely shaking in my shoes, heart pounding in my chest, but feeling good because I had done it. I had got away from the violence once more and I was used to running away because I had done it many times before, but it didn't make it any easier and I seemed to always be frightened because I was making such a mess of my life. Well, I was quite a way from Soho now but also realised that I had to hang around all day until around eleven o'clock that night before I met my toyboy. The fear was leaving me now. I was nowhere near Soho and knew that no one would be trying to find me away from there. I was walking up and down the streets of a place called Mayfair, which seemed quite posh compared to the middle of the west end. I began to feel a lot safer now, and was enjoying the warm weather, and was daydreaming as I strolled through the streets. Suddenly, a black London taxi pulled up next to me and the driver leaned his head out of the window and asked me if I wanted to make some easy money. He told me he had a client that was looking for a pretty girl to have sex with and he was famous and wanted this Taxi driver to find someone for him. The taxi driver stopped for me because I looked well dressed, sexy and nice. He told me I would be paid quite a bit of money and if I said yes, then he would drive me to his address and made me promise to be very discreet about everything. *OKAY!* I thought. There was some decent money to be made and it all seemed very genuine. Climbing in the cab, the taxi pulled off and drove for just a little while and pulled up outside a very posh but quaint house in a little side street somewhere. He got out and went up to the door and rang the bell, beckoned to me to come to the door and wait, and with that he drove off. A young-ish man answered the door and told me to come in. He was slim, decent looking, had shoulder-length hair and his face was very familiar. He was to do with pop music and I knew I had seen him sing on top of the pops but couldn't put a name to the face. He seemed very quiet, showed me to a bathroom in this very posh little house, told me to take a bath, and come to him next door into his bedroom. *Very hush-hush,* I thought to myself and didn't talk. I was nervous. I walked into the bedroom naked and he was lying on the bed just staring at my body. He asked me to sit across the top of him. He seemed very nice but was very quiet and all the time I kept thinking to myself, *where have I seen this bloke before.* I knew that I had seen him on top of the pops, I also knew that he was a singer but couldn't think of his name but I complied and did what he said. He was gentle with me so I wasn't scared at all. He didn't scare me and I trusted him, just so long as he wore protection. I was in luck; after he got an erection, he put on a condom and we had sex. It was simple as that. I was with a stranger so to speak and he just wanted a girl. It was soon over, and he treated me with respect but didn't talk much. He told me to get dressed, and he gave me £100 quid and told me to find my own way out, which I did because he hardly spoke any words at all at any time. Well, I left, money in my jacket pocket and he didn't even come out of the bedroom. *So much for that*, I thought but, once outside the door and counted the money, I was happy as Larry. Now I could walk around all day, waiting for my toyboy from Hungary, and could afford to have a meal and drink and rest when I wanted to. Wow! That was the easiest and quickest money I had ever made and nor had it been taken from me. But I can assure you and promised myself, it would never happen again and boy! Did I know that man from somewhere?

That money made my day easy and I was not near Soho so I felt happy for once and could relax. As night drew near, I made my way to Russell Square where I had arranged to meet my young man and he turned up at 11:30 pm after work. We went to his place and as he opened the door, He shushed me and told me not to utter a word and creep up the stairs behind him to his room as the landlady lived on the premises. I was as good as my word and got into his room safely. We slept together that night and it was great because he knew what I wanted and that made me happy. It was like this for a few nights, until I got caught by the landlady and we were both told to leave. Oh, bloody hell, I felt so sorry, especially for Jeno (yes I did find out his name, eventually). He was a bit pissed off with the situation but did tell me that there was another Hungarian restaurant in Queensway looking for chefs and there was a room empty over the top and he also knew the owner. We both went on the tube train to Bayswater Road, and walked to the restaurant. I waited for him outside while he went in to talk to the owner. Jeno came out smiling and told me we got the room, and he could start work in the restaurant the next day. We moved in that day and I realised that I needed a job of sorts. Well, there were plenty of ads in the paper and I found one agent who was looking for striptease dancers to work in clubs and pubs outside the West End, so I started working for this lady agent who sent me all over the place, mainly to pubs on the fringes of London. I was going to and fro on tube trains to different jobs every time she rang me with work. Things were fine for months and then we decided to move again to somewhere better. One of Jeno's friends had told him there was a really nice flat available in Streatham. We went to look at it and it was modern and nice so we decided to move again. To get to work, all he had to do was jump on a bus to go to Queensway and I had decided to go back stripping once again. I would only do my English clubs because they were safe for me and also, it had been a long time away from the pimp, so maybe he had got someone else. Don't get me wrong, I loved the pub work but travelling home on the tube late at night was awful. The trains were always full of drunks and they scared me. I just loved doing striptease, it was in my blood and Jeno asked for his old job back as a chef on Dean Street, and the boss had him back without question. We both finished work late every night and so that we could catch the bus home together, we decided to meet up in a little bar near Tottenham Court Road. Well, one night I was sitting in the comer of the bar alone waiting for Jeno and music was playing and this little Spanish guy staggered over, wanting me to dance with him. He kept pestering even though I kept saying NO! And pulled me up by my arm. Well that set my anger off big time and I did no more than pull my little penknife from my bag and with one quick swipe of my hand, I cut him across the throat and no one noticed at first and he was so drunk he didn't feel anything, but as I went to leave, the screaming started and Mr Spanish just looked down at his feet and saw his life's blood dripping out from the bottom of his jeans. As I ran out the door, I bumped into Jeno and we just strolled across the road to catch the bus home and I told him the whole story of what just happened. Jeno suggested that I stay home for a few days, and he would go to work as usual.

'Okay, I will,' I promised and did stay at home.

It took the police a whole week to find me, and I knew that they had by the sound of the banging on the front door. I let them in and told them I knew why they were there and was arrested on the spot for committing an act of grievous bodily harm. They read me my rights and took me in their police car to West End Central Police Station, where they locked me in a cell. I was kept in that cell, after I had made a statement, for a whole bloody week before I was told I was going to go to Marlborough Street Magistrates court the next day. The police were nice to me but I knew I was in deep shit. Well, the court date arrived and I was feeling very frightened. My stomach was churning and I felt sick in my stomach. The police took me in a black Mariah as they were called in those days and to the Magistrates court. I was taken to the cells underneath the court and had to wait for my turn in front of the judge. It was one big cell and there were girls there, that were equally as scared as me. One was being sick with nerves, one didn't give a shit and was happy and I just stood in a comer, away from all of them.

Eventually, my name was called up and I had to walk up that long set of stairs from the cells until I was told to sit in the court with two officers by my side. The judge read out the charges and I was in a complete daze. I really did not know what was going on and my duty solicitor seemed pretty amateur, but the judge conferred with the information he had got and told me to stand. I looked over my shoulder but through my tears did not see anyone I recognised. The judge was very stern, and although the victim I had hurt did not show up in court (the twat had already gone back to Spain), the police had photos of his neck and scars and the judge did no more than give me six months in Holloway prison. I wasn't allowed to speak and the judge said, 'Take her down.'

That was it, I was going to a bloody prison. I could not understand why the judge gave me that sentence, because all the police had to show was photographs of the idiot's scar and he had already gone back home but I was charged with grievous bodily harm and the swine of a judge was tough that day and seemed to be in a bad mood so the police took me back down to the cells to await transport to prison. Six fucking months for defending myself. I was in a bloody daze and very scared. I was taken back to the cells where there were women who were going crazy and I was really frightened. Eventually, we were called to go out of a side door into a long black police van. To be honest, I was shitting myself. I was scared and didn't know what to expect. We girls were put into individual little kiosks, which did have a window to look out of, and as I gazed out at the streets going by, I pined for those streets, to be walking them again, and the fresh air which I was denied and eventually, we arrived at the gates of the original Holloway Prison. I remember the gates opening and closing behind us. I didn't know what to expect and was so very scared. We were taken out of the police van after it stopped and ordered to walk to the reception room. I realised I had lost my freedom for six whole months and felt empty inside. Now I had to be prepared to abide by the regulations of the system and there was nothing I could do. In reception, in those days, in 1975, things were basic and archaic and old-fashioned. We were ordered to get in line and eventually ordered into the doctor's room to be examined all over including internally. My head was fucked but I complied with the orders. A big butch doctor told me to lie on a table and spread my legs and examined me internally. God knows why she did this. I think it was because she enjoyed it but she was brutal and I hated the feeling of pain I got.

She seemed to get pleasure out of it though. Maybe she was a lesbian and enjoyed her job but she was a cruel bitch. After us girls had all gone through this, we were ordered to stand in line and wait for the issue of some prison clothes. This included some knickers, shoes, trousers and sweaters. That was it. When all that crap was over, we were all ordered our different cells. I was put on D Wing floor and had to share a cell with a very young girl who was in for just shoplifting.

There were bunk beds and I had the top one. I laid my things out, toothbrush and paste and soap and towel and a toilet roll. That was it. There was a bucket in the comer with a lid on and that's where we went to the toilet for a wee or a poo regardless and it stayed in there until morning. It was so basic and primal that I thought about animals and when caged, they had all their native wild instincts taken away from them. There was a window high up near the ceiling to let daylight in but apart from that, there was nothing. My cellmate, whose name was Chrissie, told me she was in for shoplifting, and also I found out she was a self-harmer who kept trying to cut her wrists with anything she could lay her hands on that was sharp. I did make friends with her and felt very sorry for her but I adjusted and life went on with me crying a lot and absolutely wrecked with everything that was happening right now but I was not sorry for what I did. I defended myself against a drunken wanker and I landed in Holloway but I wasn't sorry for what I did. He was a bastard and I hated him for groping me. Sod him! We were woken at 6 am every morning and told to slop out, where we had to stand in line and go to the sluice room to empty our buckets. Then we had to have a shower and clean our teeth, then line up for breakfast and after that, everyone was given their work rota for the day. I was told to go to the workroom, where I ended up making little figurines which I found out were then sold to tourists coming to London for sightseeing. These items were sent in boxes to shops all around London. We also got paid a small wage every fortnight and went to a little shop within the prison to buy toiletries and tobacco. Must admit, it was a scary, violent place and believe it or not, I found out that I was on D Wing, which housed Myra Hindley, the child killer.

That put the wind up me, I can tell you and I did bump into her a couple of times.

I saw a lot of violence inside that prison. There was an old lady in there that had killed her husband with a hammer, a big black lady who tried to drown herself in a bath and was a complete head case. Fights broke out on a regular basis in the television room that were really violent and this scared me so I kept my head down at all times. I refused any visits from anyone and after about four months into my sentence, I was called into the Governor's office and told that as this offence I had committed was the first time I had been in trouble, I was being transferred to an Open Prison in Stoke-on-Trent named Moor Court. I would have more freedom, there would be no bars and I would be able to work outside if I wanted to. There were no cells, instead, there were dormitories where inmates would sleep. That sounded much better than this violent place, I thought and was told I would be going to this new open prison at the end of the week. I was allowed to write a letter to my boyfriend Jeno and give him the address of where I would be going because I would not mind him visiting me there for the last two months of my sentence. The night before I was due to leave this medieval prison, I was told I would have to be put in a holding cell, away from all the other prisoners, and would be searched the next morning in case I was trying to smuggle anything out to take with me. I was okay with that because I would be on my own, which I preferred to the violence I was witnessing on a daily basis. Night time arrived and I was told to collect my toiletries and personal item, which was next to nothing and follow a prison warden to the holding room which was a little cell with a single bed and a bucket. Being locked in, I didn't mind as I knew I would be leaving the next morning. Thank God, I was getting out of here even though I still had to finish my sentence which was only another two months. A good sleep was in order after all the screaming and shouting that went on after lights out in the main prison. Morning came quickly and I washed and got ready. A warden came in and searched me and my things and I was then told to follow her.

There was a normal police car waiting on the grounds near the big huge gates to the prison. I got into the back seat and was locked in. We slowly drove out of those huge gates, surrounded by horrible high walls and I never looked back. That place had left me with too many nightmares so it was with a happy feeling that I could look out the windows of the car and see the normal world once again, going about their daily business. I have no idea where Stoke-on-Trent was but it was a hell of a long drive and then, after driving through the countryside for ages, we drove through a normal open gate and up a long drive, pulling up in front of a big huge mansion house. It all looked posh and I did notice there were no high walls, no barbed wire, and lots of rolling green fields and trees surrounding us. I was taken into the house to be met by a new warden and taken into her office. I was told of the rules and regulations and then the warden picked up her phone and asked one of the inmates to come and show me around and show me where I would be staying. At the back of the posh house, there were lots of dormitories and I would be staying in the one this girl showed me to. She pointed to a bed and said that's where I would be staying and now to follow her back to the office. I was given duties and a work schedule and was told I was allowed to work on the farm if I wanted to. That sounded great to me. *Can't be bad,* I thought, *easy last two months before I'm free and hopefully I will get a visit from Jeno.*

As I was sorting my few things out on my bed, I thought to myself, *Hang on a minute, I haven't had a period since I was arrested, and I hadn't had one since. That was four months ago.* I put it down to the stress of everything that had happened and my stomach still looked flat. I didn't feel sick or anything but asked to see the Governor Lady and ask if I could be examined by a nurse in the clinic there.

'Of course, you can. Is something wrong, my dear?'

'Well, I haven't had a period for four months and I think it might be due to stress but I'm not sure. She sent me straight to the nurse who when I told her, gave me an internal examination.

'Well, my love, I would say you are about four months pregnant.'

'Christtttt! I never thought of that, I put it all down to the stress of being in trouble and prison.'

Oh my God, I felt so happy. It would be Jeno's and if he came to visit in two weeks, I would tell him. I think the reason I was so happy was that I needed a baby to replace what I had lost when I left my first love. I needed something to fill that empty space in my arms. Well, I worked first in the workshop, then told I could work on the farm. It felt absolutely brilliant. All the fresh air and I cleaned out pig sties and fed cows and some of us girls used to hide up in the hay barns for a smoke. One day though, soon after arriving, I felt quite poorly with a stomach ache that got worse and worse as the day went on.

I sat on the toilet thinking, I wanted to have a wee but started wanting to push. I yelled out loudly for someone to come help me. It was all a haze after that. I felt something drop into the toilet, realised what was happening and the next thing I knew, I woke up in hospital with a doctor standing over me. My stomach still hurt like hell and the doctor told me I was still in labour and to push if I felt the need. Lying on the bed, I turned my head to see a warden sitting by the table.

'Fuck me, what did they think I was going to do? Escape into the unknown?'

I felt the pushing coming again and then, just as suddenly, the pain was over. I was told by the doctor that I had had a miscarriage. One in the toilet at the prison, and one just now.

'I'm sorry, my girl,' he said to me quietly.

They weren't formed properly and they were dead anyway. I had twins growing inside me and I didn't know. All this shit and stress that I had gone through was the reason this happened to me. And this shitty doctor thought it was nothing. What a callous bastard. The doctor told the warden to let me stay in bed for a day then carry on as usual and with that, I was taken back to Moor Court and put to bed. Everyone was really nice to me though so I couldn't complain. The next day, all I did was cry and I was in a totally emotional state. I suppose deep inside my heart, I had wanted those babies because I wanted a replacement for the daughters I had turned my back on and left in 1969. Maybe I just wanted a baby to fill the emptiness of what I had already lost with my first true love. All I knew though was that at the weekend, I was to get a visit from Jeno and I promised myself that I would not say anything about the pregnancies to him as it might upset him also, so I got my strength back slowly and went back to work on the farm as normal and pretended that my heart wasn't breaking inside so deep that it hurt in my heart because, after what I had gone through, I just wanted to go back to Nottingham and get my family back, knowing that it wasn't going to happen. I realised, at that moment, that I could not really love Jeno if I felt like that and stayed with him because I was lonely and maybe just needed companionship because I felt so empty inside.

Well, Saturday came and I was going to get a visit which I was looking forward to because it would break up the mundane routine of prison life. All visitors were ushered into a big room and all the girls getting visits, were lined up, then allowed to enter the hall and make their way to their respected visitors. I spotted him straight away and went and sat next to him, a big smile on my face. This was the first time I had seen him since I was arrested in London and it was good to sit with him. He told me that he had moved jobs and now worked in Liverpool, which was closer to Stoke-on-Trent than London and that he was living in a bedsit and would be at Liverpool station waiting to meet me when I was released. Fantastic news for me and we carried on catching up with our news knowing that in about three weeks, I would be finishing my sentence and be free. The visit ended and although we were not allowed to touch, I did manage a quick hug from him.

'See you in two weeks,' he whispered, smiling because he knew I would be with him the week after that.

I walked back to my dorm, smiling. Everything was going to be okay for me now and I'm sure of that and another request was made to me by a lot of the girls. Most of them had heard that I was a stripper, and asked me if I would do a strip for them in the annexe library. *Okay, why not*, I thought to myself and the night before my release, they put all the tables together and they found some music for me. It was "I believe in miracles" by Hot Chocolate.

Bloody good song that, I thought. Well, it was so funny in a way because although I wore my own clothes, but the underwear was a traditional prison issue. Well, I kid you not, one girl was the lookout at the door, music was put on and I jumped up on the tables and as the music started, I started dancing and taking my clothes off whilst doing my sexy dance on the tables. The girls were clapping and shouting 'get em off' and I did just that, with the exception of the big baggy knickers I was wearing, which were so embarrassingly large that I rolled them down quite a bit. I enjoyed dancing around on those tables, completely naked at the end and the girls giving me wolf whistles. We made it without getting caught and I went to bed that evening in yet another holding cell ready for my release the next morning and was allowed my own clothes to wear. I was told I would be taken to Stoke railway station and the warden would buy me a single ticket to wherever I wanted to go. I told them, 'Liverpool, please,' as I knew that Jeno was going to be there to meet me. Two wardens stayed with me on the platform until the train arrived and left when the train pulled out to take me far away from prison. I really could not get used to being around the public and sat in a carriage alone with my head down.

Chapter Six
Freedom

It was a really short journey, probably a couple of hours and then the train was pulling into the station. I felt happy but frightened at the same time. I could not get used to the crowds, the smells, and the pushing and shoving. When you are incarcerated, I think a person becomes institutionalised and settles down to the inside of four walls, so I found it all very strange, even though I had only been locked up for six months. Slowly walking along the platform, I kept looking and looking and eventually saw the familiar face of Jeno, smiling and holding a bunch of flowers and I just ran into his arms where I felt safe for the first time in a long time. We left the train station and I just gazed at everything around me. I followed him onto a local bus and in ten minutes we were at his bedsit. As he opened his door, my eyes met a room full of flowers and a table full of booze. *Well, what a homecoming this has turned out to be,* I thought to myself, and then felt even worse because he told me he had to go to work at his new restaurant and suggested I get settled in, then go have a look around Liverpool city.

Well, a quick kiss and he had gone and I was alone until he came home that night. I decided to explore a little bit and as I took the spare key he had left me, I wrote down the name of the street where I would be living with him, the door number, walked out the door, and walked into Liverpool. I must say that I was impressed with all the sights, but soon got tired and still felt uncomfortable around crowds so decided to wander back to my boyfriend's bedsit. Getting back and into the room he lived in, I looked around and decided that I didn't really like it or the city at all, so I opened a bottle of beer, then another one, and another and just lay on the bed and got drunk, very drunk. I yearned for London where I knew I could get work and I actually ached to be back there and not where I was. Well, Jeno came home late from work and found me quite pissed and crying and I told him I wanted to go back to London. I fell asleep in his arms and he just held me. No sex, no nothing. I didn't want to and I was too drunk anyway. Awoke the next morning, me with the hangover from hell, and him just smiling at me. I think he knew that I wanted to go back and I would not be happy in Liverpool and so he made a suggestion that we live right outside London and I could go back to Soho and work and he would find himself a qualified job in a restaurant. Jeno told me just to stick it out for the week in Liverpool while he handed in his notice and in the meantime, he would get in touch with his mum and dad down in London and ask them to look through the newspapers and see if there was anywhere away from the city that we could rent and then we could commute back and forth to London to work. Well, his dad worked quickly because within days, Jeno had some good news. His dad had found a new build three-bedroom, unfurnished house in Rainham in Kent. Never heard of it, but my boyfriend phoned the estate agent down there and arranged a deposit without seeing the bloody house and within a few days, we had packed up our stuff and were on our way back down south. We had to catch a train from Victoria station in London and travel to Rainham in Kent. I really felt like a gipsy now, always on the move but a roof over our heads was better than nothing. We found the house, yes it was brand new, so new in fact that it didn't have anything in it. Massive rooms, bare floorboards, and sod all else. Don't get me wrong. It was nice and modern but where was the money going to come from to furnish it?

Well, Jeno had a plan. He borrowed some money from his dad, and we furnished it on the same day we lived in it. Must admit, it was very basic at first but we got things together slowly. He decided to work from an agency who sent him to different parts of London to work in restaurants, and I went to Soho with some trepidation because I really was frightened of bumping into the Maltese Wanker again in case he hurt me but I decided to work just two English clubs if they would have me back. I need not have worried as the Playboy Club welcomed me back with open arms and so did the Dolls House. Those two clubs were the only two I stayed in and were not far apart and as for that Maltese bastard, he seemed to have vanished from the face of the earth, thank God!

Well, for a few months, I left work and travelled back to Rainham but at Victoria train station, I had become friendly with one of the railway police. *Here I go again,* I thought to myself. I could tell he fancied me and in a funny way, I fancied him too. I wrote down my address in Rainham and he gave me his phone number and when I told him that my boyfriend worked away, sometimes for two or three nights at a time, I told him I would get in touch and he could come to visit me. It wasn't too long before I had that chance, so basically, I could not have been in love all that much with Jeno, could I? Yet again, I was getting restless, and alone a lot of the time in a half-furnished house.

One night, on the way home I was chatting away to the policeman on the railway platform and told him that I was going home to an empty house, and he could stop by when he came off duty to see me. He agreed that he would pop and see me when he was off duty in the early hours and I said yes straight away. I didn't know where Jeno was, I knew that he was working hard because he was paying the rent and all the bills and I knew he would not be home for a day or two. I just caught my train and went home to this half furnished, unfinished house and went to bed. It must have been 3 am in the morning when I heard a tap-tap on the door. Went downstairs in my bra and pants, thinking it was Jeno coming home from one of his jobs, and when I opened the door, lo and behold! It was my policeman friend, calling to see me on his way home to Faversham, just a little bit further on down the train line. I invited him in and that was it, I or rather we were at it, on the kitchen table, on the floor and eventually in bed. I didn't really know him that well but the sex was great.

In the early morning daylight, I awoke to a motorbike pulling up outside and knew instantly who it was. Bloody hell, he was back earlier than I thought. I shook David awake and told him to get dressed quickly as the boyfriend was back from his agency work so be quick about it. Could not think straight and we barely made it downstairs looking half decent and in walked Jeno. Just one look told me that he knew what I had been up to and turned and drove off on his bike to God knows where, saying he would be back in a bit. Bloody hell, I'm really in the shit now but I really was not happy there and I was not really getting on with Jeno because he was hardly ever there.

Well, David suggested I move in with him down in Faversham. He said he lived in a bungalow and was divorced. Didn't take me long to think about that. I packed up all my belongings and trawled off to the train station before the boyfriend came back. *Here I go again,* I thought to myself, the travelling gipsy was out yet again and the feelings of not being happy were back full force so off I went. I did not even look back and I did not even feel guilty about leaving. Maybe prison life had done that to me and also because I was now one of the top strippers in Soho, I yearned to go back there all the time. I fancied my policeman but didn't love him. It was purely sex-driven. We boarded the train and as we travelled he happened to mention that he also was bringing up three kids single-handed as his wife had left him.

Whoa!!! That was a bloody big shock that I was not expecting. There were two boys and a girl, all teenagers. Must admit, I was not prepared for this but decided to give it a go anyway. Can't be more unhappy than I had become with Jeno and his never being at home. Arriving at his bungalow I thought, *well, very nice.* Maybe I could now settle down for a bit (I don't think so). Met the children who eyed me suspiciously, and settled in for the duration. Well, I can assure everyone, that duration didn't last long. A few weeks maybe. I found myself washing and ironing, cooking food for the kids who were all little bastards by the way. And I was still commuting to my work as well. One weekend I had time off, I looked around the little village of Faversham and thought to myself, *where is the nearest pub?*

I knew I could not live like this much longer. I ached to get back to Soho where a part of me belonged. Found this little country pub and went in, sat at the bar, and ordered myself a little bottle of Barley Wine. Does anyone remember how strong that was? Just sat there looking despondent and miserable and the manager of this pub came up and started a conversation with me. His name was Steve. *Oh God, not another one.* My heart was still broken from my first who I think I was destroying myself over. This Steve was nice. He had shoulder-length mousey brown hair, was a big heavy-set bloke who spoke with a cockney accent. As the pub wasn't busy, he spent time listening to my woes and troubles and how unhappy I was. I told him about my job as a stripper in London and he seemed impressed. I was in my twenties and he was a lot older than me, in his forties but he was a good listener and we talked a lot. I told him I was going to go back to Soho to keep working and that I was fed up with living where I was. He kept looking at me all the time, I was sitting at the bar and he made me laugh.

I carried on with my routine with David, looked after his children and every weekend, parked my arse in the pub and talked to Steve and drank barley wine.

One night, I didn't realise just how strong this barley wine was and just kept drinking it. It was so bloody funny because at some point before closing time, Steve asked the other regulars if any of them had seen me leave because I wasn't sitting on my stool anymore. No I hadn't left, I had just slid slowly off my stool and landed in a crumpled heap on the floor beside my stool. I was absolutely paralytic drunk without realising it. Steve called a taxi to take me home and pushed me onto the backseat. I just about managed to tell the taxi driver where I lived and when I arrived at the door, I fell out of the cab and into the front door of the bungalow. I crawled into bed as Mr Policeman was not home yet and passed out until the next morning. I felt like crap and would never touch another drink again after that session, but I had made my mind about what I was going to do that morning. As soon as David left for work and the kids were gone to school, I packed up my things yet again, went up to see Steve at the pub, he opened early as he was the manager, and told him I was going back to London to be close to my work. His face dropped because we had grown fond of each other so he gave me his phone number and told me when I got settled, to ring him and he would come up to London to see me for a couple of hours and spend time with me. He was such a quiet man and so gentle so I said that would be really nice. He gave me a kiss on the cheek, yes! On the cheek. Said my goodbyes and went to catch the train back to Soho. Deep in thought on the way back, I was thinking about where I was going to live! Again. A thought came into my head. My friend and stripper Julie lived in a flat by herself, over the Carnival Club on Old Compton street, but that club was run by the Maltese Mafia and I was a bit concerned I would bump into that dickhead which turned my stomach because I knew he could find me and hurt me if he wanted to because everywhere I had lived with him, he had always kept a gun on top of his wardrobe and I knew he would not hesitate to use it. I had no choice though as I was determined to keep working and keep my own money. I was told I could start work straight away but first I had to go see Julie, who lived in a flat above the Carnival Club. Walking through Soho, looking furtively over my shoulder for any signs of the prick who groomed me, I walked straight into the club and found Julie in the dressing room of the club. My luck was in, hopefully. I asked her if she still lived alone and could I come live with her for a while. She was so happy to see me and said yes, I could stay with her and we could catch up on my news as I hadn't seen her in a long time. That was that then. I moved myself and my stuff in and then went to work. I worked only three clubs now. The Dolls House, The Playboy Club and I actually got Tony the manager of the Carnival Club to give me a job there. He was Maltese and I did ask him if Frank was still around.

'No, he's gone to Malta for a while to stay with his wife.'

My heart soared and I felt happy for once, whatever happiness was. It was the beginning of 1977 and after a while, I thought about Steve in Faversham. It would be nice to see him again so I phoned him and I heard his voice and melted a little bit. He did tell me that he could only pop up to London for a couple of hours in the morning because he had to be back in Faversham to run the pub. 'That's fine by me,' I said, maybe a little too eagerly but we arranged to meet the next morning in Green Park which was near Victoria train station. I don't think I would miss spotting him as he was a burly tall bloke. We would meet at 10 am and he would only be able to stay for an hour before going back home. 'Lovely, see you then.'

Well, the next day came and I made myself look pretty and raced across Soho to Green Park and just walked up and down until I spotted him. He had a lovely smile and looked like he was pleased to see me. We sat on a park bench and he told me a bit about himself. He said he had been a baker in the army, he had a little boy with a Dutch girl who did not live with him but went back home to Holland with his child. Oh! And he dropped it into the conversation that back in Faversham, he was married to a woman much older than him. *Oh fuck! How many more times am I going to get involved with men that had another woman in their lives?* Bit of a shock that was but hey! I was used to it by now and thought nothing was going to come of this little dalliance. How wrong was I going to be! Well, time was up and he had to go open the Pub, so we kissed properly for the first time. I liked the feeling that I got from that and decided I wanted more so he said he would come and see me the next day, same place, same time. I was eager to keep seeing this man so said yes without hesitation. These meetings went on for about two weeks and things were certainly hotting up between us. I told him where I was living and that I was sharing a flat with a friend who I worked with. Well, one early morning the doorbell rang, I went to answer it and there he stood, holding a suitcase and telling me he had sneaked away from Faversham because he wanted to be with me and said he was falling in love with me and wanted to live with me. Oh my God, what is happening here? This I was not expecting at all but there was just something about Steve that made it right somehow. I invited him in and shook Julie awake. Had to explain this one to her very carefully because she had no idea I had been seeing him. Tell you what then, Julie said to me, 'He can stay here and you two can have the double bed and I will have the pull-out sofa. Just remember, he can't stay here for too long or I will get into trouble.'

That was okay with us and we seemed right together. I remember having such fun there. Every Sunday morning, I and Julie used to open the window of our flat, lean right out, naked from the waist up and flashing our boobs to the world, shouted good morning to everyone that walked by. We really had fun doing that because men in the street would just about trip over their feet looking up at us semi-naked. I'm telling you, we had no inhibitions in those days. Steve told me that he had just packed one suitcase and sneaked out of his house one morning and was never going back because he wanted to be with me so I accepted that and my stripping life carried on. He came to wait in all three clubs for me, standing in the auditorium, watching me and watching the punters, just to make sure I was safe, then walked with me to my next club. We lived on my money as he had been unable to find work right away and we did grow to love each other.

One day I was taken by surprise, Steve asked me to marry him. I wasn't engaged to him, hadn't got an engagement ring from him but I just stood in the middle of Soho and nodded my head up and down. That was a big YES from me so we took ourselves off to Marylebone Registry Office and booked an appointment for a wedding day. It was that quick and only had to wait about two weeks before we could marry in those days. I decided to buy myself a long white dress that was simple and wear my hair up in curls with small roses attached to my hair. I asked Julie to be my bridesmaid and she was over the moon. I asked Maltese Tony if I could have the day off work to go get married, he agreed but said I had to be back at work the next day. 'Okay, no probs then.'

Must admit though there was one niggly little thought at the back of my mind, *Oh shit, he's still married, we might get arrested or worse, PRISON*. He didn't seem bothered though as we were a long way from Faversham so that day, I dressed in my long dress, Steve wore a brown suit and with Julie tagging along, got a taxi to the registry office and got married. He put a little gold band on my finger, paid for by me but it didn't bother me and we were suddenly man and wife. Julie threw some confetti over us while we stood on the steps and then decided to get a taxi to a little pub on the corner of Old Compton Street. We did get a bit drunk, Julie was very drunk and in her posh frock had to go outside and she was very sick all over the pavement. Well, we all went back to the flat. There was no wedding reception, no wedding cake. No, nothing but I was now a married woman and I don't know how I felt. Was I looking for stability, was I looking for something to fill that hole in my heart from my younger years? I really didn't know then but I was happy that day. One thing bothered me though. We never took any precautions when we had sex but every month my period turned up and yet again, another disappointment. I really did want a baby. Maybe that was because of what I had lost or maybe because I wanted a baby with my new husband. I carried on working but had decided to make an appointment at St Mary's Hospital in Paddington to see what was going on with my insides. I had an examination and a scan and an internal and was told I had blocked damaged fallopian tubes and I needed an operation to unblock them to give me any chance of having a baby. I was booked in as soon as possible and as it was just an overnight stay, my clubs understood and held my jobs for me. I went into St Mary's Hospital under my consultant Mr Pinker, little did I know that he was to become, many years later Lord Pinker and he also had delivered all the Royal babies, even Prince Charles and many after that, but he also worked and taught in the same hospital for many years and treated ordinary women as well as royalty. I turned up for my overnight stay and on an empty tummy, was put under anaesthesia and operated on. The man himself operated on me, going through my tummy button and doing what was necessary and I came out of my anaesthesia after a couple of hours, feeling a little uncomfortable but okay. The following morning, Mr Pinker came to check on me and told me that my tubes had been badly scarred and he had cleaned them out and I should not have any problems with fertility now and could go home that day but to take it easy.

I felt okay the next day and went back to work on doing my shows. I had to go back to the hospital in four weeks, just for a check-up. I felt fine and we had sex, carefully but normally. Four weeks came around quickly, and I had also missed my first period after the surgery. Mr Pinker came and examined my tummy, looked at the scar and was quite happy that I was healing well. After telling him that I had missed one period and with eyebrows raised, told me that if I missed a second one, to make an appointment with his secretary to go back to see him in five weeks' time and he would check me again. *Well, that's a turn up for the books,* I thought to myself but did not get my expectations up. Went back to work and at that time, decided to find a place to live by ourselves as we felt we had inconvenienced Julie for too long and needed to be on our own. We scouted the local paper, The Evening Standard and did find some rooms to let in a hostel, in Paddington, just down the road from the hospital. We went to have a look and were shown to a room in this big building that housed drug addicts, winos and weirdos. One room, shared kitchen, shared bathrooms and toilets. *You have to be bloody joking,* I thought as we just looked at each other in shock horror.

Well, we took the room as it was cheap but I damn well knew that we wouldn't be there for long if it was left to me. We moved our stuff in and I carried on working as normal. Five weeks passed and so did my next period so off we went to the hospital. Mr Pinker came in and we shook hands. He asked how I was feeling and I told him I was fine, but I had not had another period. I looked at him with some trepidation and he just smiled at me and suggested he examine me, and also, could I do a wee sample, please? Off I went to wee in a cardboard container and first he tested that and then told me to go behind the curtain, lie on a bed whilst he examined me internally. I noticed he was still smiling and told me to get dressed and come sit next to my husband.

'Well, Mr and Mrs Holt, I can definitely tell you, Hazel, that you are pregnant!'

I jumped up out of my chair and ran around his desk and kissed him on the cheek, saying, 'Thank you,' over and over and over again. He just laughed and said he was glad I was happy but that was his job, to make women able to have babies and he stayed at that hospital for many years doing just that, for ordinary women as well as royal ones. As me and my husband got outside the hospital, we held each other and jumped up and down in the street. I was so happy. Maybe I can fill that emptiness that I had felt for the last few years, fill that hole and stop my heart from hurting. After calming down, I went to work as normal and I worked on stage until I was three months pregnant, going back every night to that dirty shithole hostel that felt like a den of thieves. I hated it there and I bought up the subject of leaving London behind and going back home to Nottingham. I felt like I wanted to go to be near my mum when I had this baby. We both talked far into the night about it and came to the decision to pack all we owned, for me to pick up my last week's wages and then vanish back to Nottingham, never to go back to London again, and that's just what we did. We went to St Pancras station with a one-way ticket and were soon on our way back to Nottingham, but with no idea where we were going to live. Arriving at Nottingham train station, it felt so good to be back on my home ground. We walked up maid Marion Way and found a cafe on the corner of Friar Lane in town. Buying the local newspaper, over cups of tea, Steve started looking in the Letting column and we came across a room for rent in a house on Gregory Boulevard. We decided to go and see it straight away. I think we both felt like homeless urchins right now so let's hope our luck would be in. The address was right opposite Forest Fields where they held the Goose Fair every year, and just down the road was Hyson Green. Well arriving at the address, I knocked on the door tentatively, fingers crossed. A nice lady opened the door and introduced herself as Jean, the landlady and explained that she and Ivan, her husband, owned the house and rented it out mainly to long-distance lorry drivers but offered to show us the room anyway. It was a really old house and was three stories high. Well, we climbed and climbed and climbed and finally got to the very top floor. We were let into a room that was really so small you could swing a bleeding cat around and that would be the size of it. There was a bed, a wardrobe and a table and two chairs Oh! And we had to share a shower and toilet with our next-door neighbour who was a lorry driver but at weekends was a complete pisshead. The kitchen was on our floor but the shower and toilet were one floor down. *Fuckin great*, I thought, *just fuckin great.* Another shithole, not much better than the last one but we took it as the rent was cheap and I could pay for it until Steve could find a job, which didn't take long, I might add. Before working as manager of a pub, he had the experience of working at a sewage farm and he found an ad in the paper one day and a sewage filtering farm at Stoke Bardolph, near Netherfield, so he phoned up and got a day for an interview. Because of his experience, he got the job right away. It was a long way from where we were living, including two long bus rides, but he got the job and started almost right away. The only downfall was that it was shift work. Mornings, afternoons and nights. Oh crikey, I was going to be left on my own for long lengths of time alone with nothing to do. Well, I let Steve get on with his job and I adjusted by finding my local ante-natal clinic and registering for the care I was going to need in future. I was getting fatter and started going to second-hand shops to buy frocks and trousers that fit over my tummy. I loved stroking my stomach and felt a kind of fulfilment that had been missing from me for a very long time. I loved my "bump" and loved wearing maternity clothes, what I didn't like was the stairs I had to navigate all the time. Although the landlord and landlady were very nice, they did not do much upkeep of the house. The shower and toilet were quite disgusting, well, there were about 15 lorry drivers there and hygiene was at an all-time low. Also, the stair carpet was old and threadbare and there were three floors of that to go up and down every day. I enjoyed myself there even though I was bored. My pregnancy progressed and I got huge. My belly got huge and I was so slim that I thought I was going to burst. I used to go up to the bus stop on Mansfield road and when I knew that Steve was coming off the bus, I stood there waiting for him with my huge belly sticking out. I was so proud. Maybe this would fill the empty hole in my heart from losing my first three daughters, I don't know how I felt but was so very proud of feeling pregnant.

It was 1979 and I knew I had not much longer to wait. One day, Ivan the landlord came and offered me a job. He had another house right across from the one where we were living and asked if I would like to go across and cook a full breakfast for the lorry drivers early in the morning. I jumped at the offer as I was bored shitless right now. I started the next morning, six o'clock on the dot. There was a kitchen with all the cooking utensils and so I started working. I was waddling around like a duck with a huge belly, cooking full English breakfast for all these lorry drivers. I did enjoy it for a while and the landlord paid me ten pounds a week for doing it. I was just fine until one early morning as I went out of my room, I slipped, or rather should say slid down the first few steps of the bloody rotten stairs and that shook me up but didn't make me go into shock, and I felt a bit bruised but carried on. I kept cooking, meeting my husband from the bus stop after work but thought I was okay and didn't say anything. (Fucking carpets.) I was about seven months pregnant at the time and as I kept cooking breakfast for the blokes, one day I felt a stabbing pain in my tummy and contractions as well. I felt all was not well and asked the landlord to call an ambulance. (Please God, not again.) It felt like déjà vu from my prison days. I so did not want to lose this baby from sliding just a few steps on rotten carpets. I was taken to the City Hospital where my ante-natal classes were anyway. I was put into an examination room and a consultant came to examine me as my tummy kept getting hard then soft then hard again. The nurse told me I may have had a jolt as I slid down the stairs but she did not want me to go into labour at seven months, so the doctor decided to put me on a drip to take the pains away and close my cervix as a safety measure. I was kept in a room on my own and told if all was well, I could go home the next day. Although I was worried, my husband did cheer me up when he came to see me. He bought me a packet of cooked sausages, and I just had to smile because every so often he kept saying under his breath, sausages, sausages. It was so funny. I must admit though, I did start to feel better and felt fine the next day and after I was examined, was told I could go home but take it easy and watch those stairs, which I did. It was August 1979 and I only had two more months left before my baby would be born. I had an idea that on Steve's day off, I would like to take him to see my mum and dad.

Nothing strenuous, just a couple of bus rides to Kimberley and back home. I hadn't seen my mum for a few years while in London so to see her again would be nice. I had no idea how she would react but was looking forward to a few hours away from our room. Walked up the alley and through the back gate and knocked then just walked in. The surprise on her face was noticeable and she gave me a gentle hug.

'I've brought someone to see you and to let you know that you are going to be a grandma.'

'Well, I can see that,' she replied, looking at my huge belly.

'I would like to introduce you to Steve, my husband. We got married in London but we have come back to Nottingham to stay. Where's Dad?' I asked, looking around.

'I'm afraid I've got some sad news for you. He died in 1972. He had cancer of the throat.'

Well, my life stopped there and then. My head in turmoil. I was in shock and was completely speechless. Guilt swept over me like a tidal wave. I was living with that bloody gangster at the time and working and had not contacted my parents for a very long time. I blamed myself that day and still do now. I should have been with my dad here, not down London, working for that Maltese pimp. We decided to stay the night at Mum's and I cried until there were no tears left. I slept fitfully that night but the strangest thing the next morning was what my husband said to me. He asked if my dad wore a white shirt and had held his trousers up with braces. 'Yes, always when he was home,' I told him. 'Why???'

'Well, I woke up in the night and I saw this man standing at the bottom of the bed dressed just like your dad. He didn't speak but it felt like I had his approval by marrying you.'

My eyes filled with tears but made him promise not to say anything to Mum. The next day, we had to go home back to our room! It was work for Steve that day. It was October 1979, the month my baby was due. I was just about ready I can tell you. I took it easy and no more cooking breakfast and I was very careful going up and down three flights of stairs, as I was so bloody HUGE! Bob the lorry driver and pisshead was really a very kind man, although a bit scruffy and one day when Steve was on afternoons and the Goose Fair came into town on the forest opposite where we lived, I was a bit fed up and as Bob was not driving that day, I asked him to take me over to Goose Fair.

Well, the sight of both of us, me waddling like a duck, holding onto the arm of this skinny greasy haired little lorry driver. Shocked him to the core when I asked him to wait while I had a ride on the merry go round horses. Bob's mouth dropped open and told me I was so huge, I would never get on one. With sparkly eyes, I turned to him and all I said was, 'Just fuckin' watch me,' and I did get my leg over (so to speak), and had a lovely ride going 'round and 'round and up and down on a beautiful golden horse. That was all I wanted and was my fix for the day. It made me feel energised and happy and when Steve came home from work, he just thought I was mad but laughed at me just the same. It was a strange day but was going to be even stranger the next day because I slowly went into labour and I phoned an ambulance to get me to the City Hospital. I only felt a little uncomfortable but knew that at some point I would be bringing a new life into the world.

Once at the hospital, I asked one of the staff to phone Steve and tell him to leave work and come to the hospital. I was dilating slowly but surely and the pains were getting stronger. By the time my husband arrived, I was on the gas and air and wanting to push and it was hurting like hell and I was swearing like a miner. I kept pushing but I was having a hard time. My little body couldn't do this.

Chapter Seven
Struggling to Be Born

It seemed like I had been having contractions for hours, which I probably had but this baby did not want to come out. I was examined at regular intervals, and I was growing tired, but then the doctor came and examined me down below and told me he could see the top of the baby's head and told me on the next push, he was going to use forceps to ease the baby out. Well in 1979, the forceps were a bit basic, not like the technology of today. I would describe them as being like salad spoons but metal and the doctor decided to give this baby a helping hand by introducing the forceps inside my vagina, each spoon going around my baby's head and was told to push like hell on the next contraction. I felt it coming and putting my chin on my chest, pushed like hell. Oh God, it hurt like hell and I could feel the doctor pulling and pulling. Finally, my baby's head was out and then the shoulders and the rest was easy. I heard the cry straight away and after the delivery, I found out we had a baby boy. Our first and my only son. How precious he was. They cleaned him up, brought him to me and put him in my arms and the colour of him astounded me. He was bright orangey-yellow all over with jet black hair. I was told he had Jaundice and noticed he had a bruise on either side of his head from where the forceps had gripped him to pull him out of me. I had also been ripped down below while he was struggling to come out. Bloody salad spoons that were positively medieval. I was happy now it was all over and my baby was safe in my arms with a smiling husband looking on. Thinking about it, Mr Pinker had done a good job doing that first operation on me in London. God bless him. If he hadn't done what he did, I wouldn't have been able to give life to this new little human being. We named him Michael Anthony Ronald Holt and he weighed in at just under 9 lb.

That was huge for a little skinny girl like me. No wonder he got stuck. I was allowed home from the hospital after two days. My son was born on October 22,

1979. I must admit that it took some getting used to, looking after a newborn again, especially after losing my three daughters and the first love of my life to my own stupid actions all those years ago. After I got home and settled into a routine with the baby, all the lorry drivers that lived in those stupid bedsits like us, all came to gaze at him and cuddle him and I felt so proud. Another bit of good news we received when the baby was nearly six months old was because my hubby had been offered a two bedroomed flat for us, nearer to where he worked which was Netherfield in Nottingham. We jumped at the chance, just to be able to get out of that one room in that house that was falling to bits. It was a brand new flat and to get to it you had to climb some risky outside stairs but hey! This was heaven compared to where we had been living. We didn't have much to move, just clothes and a baby's cot. Steve had some money saved and we went around the local shops and first had some carpet fitted all through, then went searching for furniture. We both made it look quite nice and I made one good friend, Sharon opposite me who had a son about the same age as mine.

Steve carried on working shift work and my son was around six months old and I found it hard work looking after him. The flat began to look nice and I was kept busy looking after my son. Luckily, the few shops were not so far away and also a dentist and doctor's surgery which I got us all registered at. Something happened that day that put the fear of God into me yet again. We were both walking towards the shops, with Michael in his buggy. He was around six months old at the time. As I was looking in the shop windows, I just glanced over my shoulder and FEAR! Total fear took over. I saw him crossing the road, a long way away from me, but he was there, in his silver silk suit, looking for me and I knew he had come to find me and if he did, he would kill me. It was my nightmare from London. The evil, mafia bastard who took all my money was here in Netherfield but the question was, how the fuck did he find me and for what??? I had to do some quick thinking here. We kept walking and I told Steve to go to the betting shop for a bit as he loved to gamble on the horses. He was fine with that and off he went. He loved his horse racing gambling. At the same time, I had to think quickly on my feet here. I found a telephone box and rang Sharon, who lived on the opposite side of the street to us. I asked if anyone had knocked on her door and she said yes, there had been a well-dressed man asking about me and where I lived. She didn't tell him where I lived but told him that I was going to be at her house in a couple of hours to celebrate her young son's birthday and I was bringing my son to her house so the two boys could have some fun together as they were both six months old but it was only Robert's birthday. I told her I would be there soon as it was past lunchtime and, in the meantime, popped into the betting shop and told Steve I was going to see Sharon as it was her little boy's birthday and that I would see him at home later, knowing he would be there for a few hours yet. I decided to take myself off to her house quickly, sneaking up and down all the back streets instead of staying on the main high street because I did not want to bump into "HIM" and to be quite honest, I was terrified of what was happening. All these thoughts were racing through my head, how did he know I was here? Although someone in Soho must have told him I had gone back home to Nottingham, no one knew we were here in Netherfield unless he had paid my mother a visit, oh, Christ, I hope not but right then, I had more pressing issues going on. If anyone had seen me that day creeping around the back streets, looking furtively over my shoulder all the time hoping to God I didn't bump into him. It could have been laughable if it wasn't so serious.

Anyway, I managed to get to Sharon's house without incident and was there by 1 pm. She had a tablecloth spread out on the living room floor and it was covered in cake and finger foods and jelly and she had put balloons around the walls. We sat both our babies on the floor and let them tuck in and get messy and have fun and waited. I was so bloody frightened, I was shaking. I sat on the floor with the kids and just clock watched, my heart racing with fear, not knowing what to expect. Spot on 2 pm, there was a tap tap tap on the door. I whispered to Sharon that if anything happened to me, phone the police. She nodded and went to open the door and asked him to come in, and standing against the wall, there he was, the man of my nightmares. I sat close to my son on the living room floor, scared to move. He said, 'Hello,' and asked if Michael was my little boy and I just whispered yes. He then asked if I was okay, not taking his eyes off me, then he asked if I was coming back to London. I immediately said no, and that I was married now and I had my son. He just stood there looking at me, not smiling, not doing anything, just standing there in his fancy silver suit. I told him I would never go back to London again and that my life was now here where I was staying to bring up my son. I never took my eyes away from his, waiting to see if he pulled a gun or came towards me to hit me, I just didn't know. Sharon stayed close to me, and I think he got the message because he just said, 'Okay then,' opened the door and left. We both listened at the closed door and heard him drive away.

I told Sharon to lock the door and just sat back down on the floor and cried and cried with relief. The man was dangerous and unpredictable and I hoped to God he would not ever come looking for me again. After that visit, I think I would be on edge for a long, long time to come. Well, the kids enjoyed the rest of the afternoon then it was time for me to quickly cross the road and go home. I had to clean my son up, get dinner ready and just try and relax and wait for Steve to come home. I also had to pretend like nothing ever happened and I never told him about it and after that day, I never saw the gangster man again. It felt like a big burden had just been lifted from my shoulders so hopefully, our life could go back to normal, which it did and life carried on as normal. When our son was about one year old, he became a very difficult child to look after. He was always having temper tantrums and would not sleep at night and we were both worn out looking after him, especially as Steve was working shift work too. After weeks of constantly, crying and being awkward to manage, I took him to the doctors, because he would only sleep in our bed with us, yet he had his own room. The doctor advised that we have him put in the hospital for a couple of weeks, and they would try and train him to get used to sleeping in a room on his own and I could visit every day and go home in the evening. All went well, he slept alone in the hospital and I don't know what they did but it worked and when we bought him home, he started sleeping well in his own room.

Life for our little family settled down very well and Michael was just being a normal little boy. We gave him a little birthday party on his 2nd birthday and my mum came over for a few hours. It was a good day. As the weeks went on, I noticed I had missed a couple of periods. *Well that can't be right*, I thought to myself because when I had my last check-up with my doctor he told me that because Michael had been such a difficult birth and with the forceps delivery, I would not be able to have any more children, but at the time I didn't worry because I had a baby, and I think, deep in my heart that's all I wanted, to replace the three daughters I had deserted. Anyway, just out of curiosity, I did a wee sample and took it to my chemist and Mavis behind the counter, who was my friend took it in the back and after a couple of minutes, came back with a huge smile on her face, gave me a big hug and said quietly, 'Congratulations, you are pregnant.'

Well, I nearly dropped to the floor, but just stood there with my mouth hanging open. I thought, *how the bloody hell did this happen*? My surgeon told me I was so badly damaged inside after giving birth to Michael that I would never have any more babies. Mavis told me I was about two months gone and I just hugged her and walked out of the chemist like a fuckin robot. I mean, I was told I was infertile. We weren't taking any precautions when we had sex because I thought I was never ever going to have any more babies.

Well, I walked home in a daze, but happy at the same time, stroking my stomach and knowing that first I had to take myself off to the doctor the next day and get myself sorted properly but as for now, I had to go home and break the news to Steve, not knowing what reaction I would get. All I knew at that moment in time was walking in the sunshine, towards our little flat knowing that I had a little miracle growing inside me when I never thought I would ever have again. It took me time going back home, trying to take this news in. Thinking in my head that this wasn't supposed to happen. We had never taken any precautions against me getting pregnant again for two years and my insides had been so badly damaged inside, my womb was scarred from losing the babies in prison, I had excessively heavy bleeding with each period and was damaged with the forceps delivery of my son resulting in me having many stitches put in after the birth of my son, so it never entered my head that there would be any more pregnancies for me and I was okay with that, so this was a bolt out the blue. A little life growing inside me that wasn't supposed to be, me being about 34–35 years old and having a really difficult time with my son because as he grew, he got more uncontrollable and hard to manage, so that was a full-time job. Well as I got back home, reality had set in and I just remember walking in the door and just saying to my husband, 'I'M PREGNANT.' I will never forget the smile that came across his face as he stood in the living room, then came across to me and gave me the biggest hug.

Well, he was as gobsmacked as me so over a cuppa, I had to start making plans to go and get onto the local ante-natal list and start making plans. Of course, while this was all going on, Michael was still running me ragged and being a little shit. No matter how hard I tried to be a good mother, he had a mind of his own and would not do anything he was told and still continued being a little swine at bedtime, playing up and hardly ever sleeping in his own room which we had made really nice for him. Surely, he had to start slowing down at some point and although I tried to explain that Mummy had another baby growing in her tummy, I think he was either too young to understand or he didn't give a toss.

Well, life carried on as normal and my tummy started to get bigger and I just could not stop stroking it and protecting this baby because it wasn't supposed to be here. With my pregnancy with my son, I grew so huge I thought I would burst, especially as he was also overdue to be born, but my stomach with this pregnancy grew slowly but normally and at all my check-ups I was told all was well. I never had morning sickness and felt very healthy and my only craving at that time was Aubergines' and I sent hubby out at every chance I could to keep me stocked up with them. I love them to this day. I was only small and still skinny and just had this little bump inside me, but must admit that as I neared the end of this pregnancy I did waddle like a duck and it was summer so I did feel quite knackered. I sailed through this one with no complications and was full of energy. It's strange but women tell me that just before birth, you get an urge to clean and covet and clean the house and are full of energy all the time, well I felt like that all the time. I did notice one day though that all I felt was a heaviness in the pit of my stomach but still kept soldiering on. It was July 1982 and I always remember that I was standing at my sink washing the pots when I felt a sensation like a PLOP from my vagina into my knickers. That was really weird and I took myself off into the toilet to have a look. In my knickers was a plug of jelly and I just stood there wondering what it was and then I remembered that the same happened when I started labour with my second daughter.

That one happened in the outside toilet of the house, me and my first husband had rented where the toilet was outside and by torchlight, I saw the same thing happen so I knew this was the beginning of my labour. Well, I got my hubby to phone an ambulance and told him that I thought I was in labour but he could not come with me as he had to stay behind and look after our son. He panicked and was rushing around like a bloody banshee but to be quite honest, I felt just fine. I was taken to Queens Medical Centre in Nottingham and taken straight to the delivery room where I was made comfy in a bed with nurses checking on me nearly all the time. It didn't take long before the pains started coming and when the nurse examined me, I was told that I was nearly 9 cm dilated and it wouldn't be long now. Bloody hell, didn't think I was that far gone but no sooner had I thought that to myself, whoosh!!! My waters broke and then I knew I was on my way. My friend from over the road was there with me so I felt comforted. It was around 5pm that evening that I wanted to start pushing so the nurse gave me the gas and air thing to suck on but as the pains became stronger, I started swearing like a trooper to no one in particular and begged the nurses to give me an epidural because the pain was so intense. They refused as they said the birth was imminent. I had my friend Sharon holding one leg and a nurse holding the other.

There I was effing and blinding at my hubby who wasn't even there, blaming him for this pain and screaming that it was all his fault. I wanted to puke, then I didn't and between pushing, thought to myself that the imminent birth was taking its fucking time because it was way past that, but when the nurse said she could see the baby's head and one more last push should be the final one, I really worked hard, even though I felt I was being split in two and when the feeling came, I put my chin on my chest and pushed as hard as possible, screaming like a bloody banshee all the way and finally, the head was born and with another little push and a lot of panting, out the baby popped. I was told I had a little girl and they put her straight onto my stomach, cord completely attached, and she was crying. The emotion and tears poured out of me as I held this little human onto my stomach while the nurses tried to clean her up while I was holding onto her, they cut the cord and quickly wrapped her in a blanket and took her to be weighed and cleaned up.

My daughter weighed 7 1b 8 oz., and when they brought her back to me wrapped in a blanket, the sight of her was so strange because although she was perfect in every way, I could not take my eyes away from the shock of grey hair she had. Yes, pure grey. It was thick and long and there was a lot of it but it was GREY!!! The nurses just kept looking at her hair and thought the colour was unreal but in all, she was tiny and perfect and beautiful and a baby that was never supposed to be born at all because my womb was never supposed to hold her in there for nine months. Therefore, from that day until present, I will always regard her as my 'MIRACLE BABY' and do to this day.

While I lay there in the delivery room, the nurse bought my baby to me. My friend Sharon went home to give the good news to my hubby and as soon as I held her in my arms, I started breastfeeding her straight away, but could not take my eyes off her hair. It wasn't silver, it wasn't blonde, it was proper grey, like an old lady's. Well, the nurses had a field day because they were always brushing it into different styles. One day she looked like a punk rocker with it all pointed up and the next time it was brushed straight down nearly to her neck. Very strange but a beautiful baby and I was allowed home after only two days. It was great being home and we named our baby Kelly Ann.

Well, I introduced her to her two-year-old brother, he stroked her cheek, pushed her back into my arms and carried on playing. Think I'm going to have some jealousy problems with him but for now, I had to rest and look after this little miracle I had in my arms. I didn't feel too well because before I left the hospital, they gave me the German Measles injection for protection for me and the baby which was fine but it made me feel like shit. I went into the bedroom, closed the door and lay on the bed with my baby daughter and just gazed at this amazing little human, and this huge mop of grey hair. I tried to figure out what colour it would be as she grew but had no idea and I fell asleep with her in my arms. I awoke to her crying, realising that she wanted milk so gently put her to my breast and she started guzzling straight away. I was contented and could hear my little son in the living room, driving his dad mad as usual. I felt better after the rest and walked into the living room and handed our new born to her dad. Hubby was holding her and looking at her with pride, at the same time, I could see the tiniest glint of anger in Michael's eyes. It seemed like he hated the fact that all the attention was projected towards the new baby and he was a bit miffed, to say the least. As we all fell into family life again, things more or less carried on as normal. Kelly being a quiet little girl and Michael being a little pain in the arse. I tried to involve him in everything we did as a family and gradually he seemed to calm down for a while and peace was restored. When Kelly was about three months old, I had a letter from the council, offering us a three bedroomed house just up the road from where we lived and asked would we like to go and look at it. *Well, that's a turn up for the books,* I thought to myself and jumped at the chance.

To be honest, I wanted to move for two reasons really, one was that the flat we lived in was really too small and two was that I was still scared that the Maltese mafia groomer that had tormented me for a few years, might just come back looking for me to hurt me so the move could not have come at a better time. We all went to see it as a family and said yes to the council straight away and as soon as we had carpet fitted throughout the house, we hired a man with a van, loaded up everything and moved to a hopefully more unscary life for me. That evil man had instilled in me total fear after the years of abuse I suffered at his hands and I still looked over my shoulder many times. That's what grooming does to a girl, you adore them but also fear them so therefore you are always subservient and fearful and because he had found me once since coming back to Nottingham, who knew if he would ever show his face again. These sort of men always had ways of finding people, no matter where they were and that's what scared me at that time.

Those thoughts were pushed to the back of my mind though as we started to enjoy our new home. Life was good. I got Michael into nursery school just for half a day which was good but the little bugger would not walk to school, I had to push him to school in his pushchair, with a dummy in his gob as well and that continued until he was six years old. What a bloody embarrassment that was. Kelly started the same infant school when she was four years old and went there like a dream with no problems and by the way, her hair grew long and it turned a beautiful natural blonde colour. She was no longer a little grey-haired old lady, she had turned into a lovely little blonde beauty. She stayed at infants school for another year and when Michael was seven, he had to move up to middle school on Chandos Street in Netherfield and that's when he started being a little shit. I started getting reports that he was unruly in school, insolent to his teachers and getting out of control. Kelly moved up to the same school when she was nearly six, so it was easy for me as they now went to the same school, full time and it was lovely having some time to myself, except when I was called in to see the headmaster about Michael's unruly behaviour. How I got him out of trouble so many times, I will never know. Also, as he was growing older, I noticed he was changing at home too. He became a bully to his sister and never did what he was told. I took them both out at the weekends, on a train into town to treat them to a McDonald's and buy them toys and at that time, he was always wanting me to buy him those plastic dinosaur models, but as time went on, I watched him mutilate them, stab them with anything he could find, stabbing them and pulling their heads off and it was at this time, he started being a total bully to his sister to the point that she became very scared of him because he was so unpredictable. He punched her for no reason, kicked her and smacked her for no reason and he would not listen to anything me or his dad told him to do.

One day, he threw a pair of scissors at her which stuck in her leg. I was seriously getting worried about him because he was ranting and raging at all of us, for no apparent reason. They were both out of nursery now and both in the same school. Kelly was in the young starters classes and Mike was two years older and in the more advanced part of the school. I really did lose count on how many times I got called in to see the headmaster who was very concerned about his behaviour but I was at a loose end as to what to do with him. While they were both in school one day, I was at home enjoying some ME time and I thought Steve was at work but all of a sudden there was a tapping on the front door and when I answered it, there stood Steve, crying and bent over in agony with his back. He had been sent home because he had suffered a bad accident at work. He worked at a Sewage Plant and Steve had to dredge all the raw sewage and load it onto a train truck, to be taken away to be treated. Well, one of those trucks had tipped off the tracks and fell onto Steve and damaged his back. *Bloody hell,* I thought to myself, this was serious so phoned the doctor straight away who said he would come out and take a look at him. He was sent to the hospital where he underwent a scan and the consultant told him that his spine was fine but his hip had been badly damaged and he would need a hip replacement and would put him on the list. He arrived back home in a taxi and the hospital had given him callipers to help him walk while he waited for an operation. Well, that was a shock to my system. He was told that he would never work again and he didn't. He just went into a reclusive state and never really came out of his depression. The doctor put him on antidepressants that turned him into a bloody zombie and he just gave up. He sat in his armchair all day watching television and wanted to eat crap food like fish and chips, and choc ices and began to put on an enormous amount of weight. We both decided to sue the water authority for the accident and they quickly came back to us with an offer because they admitted it was their fault as a lot of their machinery was old and didn't work properly. They made him an offer and he accepted so we just had to play the waiting game for a while. In the meantime, I had to find a way of getting him moving so I suggested that he go and meet the kids from school every day. He had learned how to use the callipers so there was no excuse. He didn't argue with me and struggled his way to wait outside the school gates for the kids. Mike just hated it and just kept telling his mates that it was his granddad who was waiting for him. Steve sort of went grey-haired overnight and his hair was shoulder length and he was overweight, but at least he got the exercise which I hoped would help him. Kelly just loved to see her daddy outside the gates waiting for him and didn't see him as anything different but her dad.

Well, life carried on. My son hated both of us, me for making him wear clothes brought from cheap shops instead of branded ones like all his mates, and bullied me constantly because I wore things from second-hand shops, so he hated walking in the streets with me too. Kelly was a happy little girl who did not let anything bother her except she became more scared of her brother. He would cut her little Barbie dolls up into bits, he would thump her and punch her and try to hurt her in any way he could. She became really scared of him but although I tried to intervene, I got kicked and punched too and Steve never admonished him at all. He left everything to me. Occasionally, Steve got a letter from his son from his first marriage. He had never hidden the fact that he was married before and had three children with his first wife and way back before I met him, his wife had met someone else and she had decided to move with this new man to Australia and take the kids with her. He had one son and two daughters. Steve had never lost contact with his son though and got the occasional letter from him.

Meanwhile, I was about to have a very big surprise of my own one night. The kids were doing their own thing, I was watching TV with Steve and it was dark and cold outside. Suddenly, there was a knock on the door. I got up to open it and there stood a young girl, with a little boy in a pushchair. I looked and asked if I could help her and she just looked at me and said, 'Do you know who I am?'

I shook my head, 'No, I'm sorry.' Then the bombshell.

'I'm Mandy your daughter, and this is my little boy Adam.'

I just stood there with my mouth open. The last time I saw her was when she was three years old and I used to go see her with her sisters at my mum's house when I had access rights which was every two weeks when I lived in London. I told her to come inside as it was cold and she just sat on the sofa and then I had the unenviable task of telling Mike and Kelly who she was. She was their half-sister. Steve already knew about my girls when I met him but we had never told our kids because I never thought I would see them again.

I just sat next to her and gave her a hug, tears rolling down my face. There were so many questions I wanted to ask her but really just wanted to know why she had knocked on my door and what was wrong. I could not stop staring at her because she looked just like her dad, my first love. She told me that she was living in a maisonette in Nottingham, by herself, that the father of her little boy had left her and she wanted to know if she could have some money for some food as she had no one with her and was on her own. I just kept staring at her. She was about sixteen, just a kid. The same age as me when I had her. I thought to myself, *you could not make this shit up, you just couldn't.* She stayed a while longer. Kelly and Mike were just staring, Steve was just staring and I was an emotional fucking wreck. I asked her to write down her address and asked if it would be okay if I could come and see her at some point. She said she wanted to see me again so I agreed to go see her the following day and told her I would take her some food. Steve gave her some money and I sent her home in a taxi because it was dark and cold. I hugged her and cried some more and waved her off in a taxi. I never asked her about her dad or her upbringing, although I did know Stephen had met someone and she was bringing up my three daughters, but as far as I was concerned, she was a substitute and those three girls will always carry my blood inside them regardless. Well, that was a night to remember and I went to bed very emotional that night.

Well, I put Kelly into her buggy the next morning because we had two long bus rides and went to find Mandy. I had to juggle the buses but eventually got to this high rise building where I thought she lived. Got there, pressed the right buttons and went up on the lift to her flat where she lived. The door opened and there she was with this little boy. She invited me in. She hadn't got much but it was a comfy place and me and my daughter felt comfortable there. I had a big bag of food for her and although she was silent, I think she was grateful. We let the two children play and I started asking her about her life and tried to explain why I left her and her sisters but before we got talking, there was a knock on her door and in raced Stephen, my first love, said a quick hello, looked at me and raced upstairs to use the toilet. I looked and he looked just the same as when I first met him. Jet black hair, sideburns and a quiff and looked like Elvis. I just sat there with my mouth open and all the butterflies in my tummy came back again. He came downstairs, waved at me but looked at me with those eyes and left because he was working but I had a feeling he knew I was there and just turned up knowing that he would see me. I never asked Mandy about him but my heart filled with tears because I had to think about Kelly and not let my emotions show but my god, after all these years, it felt like a bullet had shot through my heart. Anyway, I stayed there for a while and then said I had to go home but I would visit her soon and bring more food. She was beautiful and looked just like her dad. I was so proud but sad at the same time. I visited her often but then one day, all of a sudden, she had gone. I went to an empty maisonette and she had left and I have no idea where she had gone and she had also left from my heart. I was broken yet again because I had no way of finding her but seeing her, with a child at sixteen, same age as me when I had her and also seeing her dad fleetingly, my heart broke yet again in many tiny broken bits but I knew I had to carry on looking after the family I had now. My brain could not rest that night and many nights after that but I knew I had to carry on looking after my two children, and I also knew that I would bump into my first love again. I had locked him away into a little box in my brain for all these years but now that box had been opened by just seeing a glimpse of him that one time, and I had a funny feeling it would not be the last.

Well, life went on as they say and I carried on being the dutiful wife and loving mother and Steve was waiting to hear from the water authority to see if he would get any compensation from them. Well, after a few weeks of waiting, a letter and a cheque came through the door and we were both gobsmacked. It was non-negotiable but it was a six-figure sum so after we calmed down, I took it into town and banked it. Steve carried on taking the kids to school, Mike hated it because he thought all his schoolmates were taking the piss out of him and kept saying to his friends that Steve was his grandad. Just because he had long grey hair and walked with crutches didn't make him any less of a man. Kelly was her usual placid little self, bless her, but once home, she was terrified of her brother because he was always bullying her. He was either cutting up all her toys, tripping her up or thumping her.

Well, what to do, what to do? I decided on a plan that would hopefully cheer us all up.

Chapter Eight
A Plan for Happiness (Maybe!)

It was 1987, Kelly was five and Mike was seven respectively, he was still being an obnoxious little bastard and Kelly was always calm except when Mike started tormenting her, then she became scared and drew into her shell, bless her. Steve was just being Steve, sitting in his armchair near the window, watching television and eating for England. He was still waiting for his hip operation and seemed to have given up. The only exercise he got was when he took the kids to school and our son was always ashamed of having to walk with him, but then again, he was always ashamed of me also. Oh! How I wish I knew what was going on in his head.

Anyway, now Steve had his compensation and I was also able to buy new clothes for the kids which made them feel better, I planned to do something far bigger and hopefully make the family a happy one again. I asked for Steve's bank card and told him I was going shopping into town for a bit while the kids were at school. He didn't argue, he was watching horse racing on the television. Probably he would hobble off down to his local bookies for a few bets. Anyway, off I went on the bus into town, heart thumping in my chest and hoping this plan would work. Jesus! It had better fucking work, I was putting my life on the line here but I was so bloody determined to try and get my family back to some normality that it had to work. I walked straight across town and right into the British Airways travel agents with a confident look on my face, I told them I wanted to book return flights to Brisbane, Australia. I asked them to make them out for two adults and two children, leaving in November and coming back in January. I can't remember the exact dates but the tickets were booked and I was informed that I would receive them through the post. The total cost of the tickets was £3000. I paid with our card and the job was done. Now all I had to do was go home and tell Steve what I had done and face the consequences. I also had to write a letter to Steve's son in Australia telling him when we were going to arrive, and also get some passports sorted out. It was July and I hadn't got much time but I was determined to reunite Steve with his son and two daughters and the rest of the family and also have a family adventure for ourselves at the same time. It may make my son a little calmer and make my little girl a bit happier because I was so bloody fed up with seeing her cowering when her brother came near her and threatened her and also it may lift Steve out of his depression he had got himself into because he knew he would never work again and he had simply given up. *Well, here goes nothing*, I thought to myself and walked straight through the front door and put a copy of the booking form into his hands and told him to read it. He read it, looked at me and read it again. 'I can't go like this with two bloody callipers,' he shouted and I told him at least he could walk and wasn't in a wheelchair. I told him he was going to meet his children and that was that and I also told him I had written to his son over there and he knew the date we would be landing and would make sure all three of his now grown-up kids, who he hadn't seen since they were little, would be at the airport to meet him. I worked it as although we would all be going in November when we would be leaving the cold weather behind, we would be staying for around two months with his son and it would be Christmas there and very very hot. That was it. He had no choice in the matter. He was going to meet the children he hadn't seen since they were small and that was that. My good deed for the day (or so I hoped).

To be quite honest, the kids were excited but he just sat looking at this form, either not giving a shit or just letting it all sink in. Well, hopefully, this will get him off his arse and have something to look forward to. He came around after thinking about it for a while and I gave him a hug and whispered, 'Don't worry, this will do you good.'

Well, I had to get my arse in gear then. Sorted the passports, packed two huge suitcases and arranged for us to get the train from Nottingham train station and then a taxi to Heathrow airport. Must admit, although I was knackered I felt that I had done something good for a change and an adventure was about to come together. I had booked a night flight because, in those days, it took about 14 hours to get there with a stopover in Bombay as it was called then, just for an hour to refuel. It was in the days when you were allowed to smoke on aeroplanes, so I was sorted. I probably would need a few after being on a plane for such a long time with two kids and a disabled husband. Got my adopted mother to take care of the house and keep checking on it and when the day arrived, I decided to let the kids travel in pyjamas for the duration because they would be sleeping through the night and I was shitting myself thinking what could possibly go wrong (it did)! But not to worry, off we went and got to Heathrow, found our plane and boarded. It was very strange for the kids but they were excited and I made sure that I had a bottle of Phenergan in my bag in case they got sick. In those days, you could bring things like liquid medicines through control and there were no restrictions. We were guided to our seats and we had the ones with plenty of room because of Steve and his callipers and also a seat each for the kids so they could sleep. We took off and I was fine with it and knew what to expect but the kids didn't. At first, they were terrified as the plane took to the skies and Kelly was sobbing, but then she relaxed along with her brother. He seemed to be quiet for a change, and as for me, I was feeling relaxed for a change, which was once in a fuckin blue moon. (I spoke too soon.)

About an hour into the flight, remembering that the kids should be asleep, and I was having a smoke at the back of the plane, a stewardess came and told me that my son was feeling ill. Went back to my seat and looked at him and he was grey and holding on to a sick bag. *Oh god help me and give me strength,* I thought to myself. Here we go! He started being sick and puked for England and it seemed to go on forever. He filled one sick bag after another and suddenly I knew I would not be sleeping any time soon. Kelly, bless her, was drawing in her book and looked quite unperturbed by him. Maybe there was a twinkle in her eye, I think it looked like a sort of "I've got you back, you little shit" twinkle.

After a few hours, we landed at Bombay airport where all passengers were allowed off the plane for an hour to stretch our legs, while the plane was being re-fuelled, so me and hubby made the best of this situation to just walk around the airport lounge so Mike could have a breather but NO! That didn't happen either. I swear, every single ashtray we walked past, Mike bent over and puked into each one of them and there were a lot of them believe you me. Eventually, we were allowed back on the plane and I must admit, I did feel a bit sorry for my son. I gave him another spoonful of Phenergan hoping to get some respite for both of us. We took off once more and he did sleep then and all of a sudden, daylight shone through our windows and we came in to land in Brisbane at last. Steve didn't talk to me much throughout the flight but just lately we haven't talked much at home anyway but maybe he was a bit scared of meeting his first family after a lot of years so I let him off with that one. Anyway, after collecting our suitcases and going through security, we walked through the corridor and through the doors at the end and there they were, all waiting for us. I instantly recognised Steve's son because he was the exact image of his dad. Tall, chubby, with a beard and almost his double. They all hugged their dad, hugged the kids, and his son just looked at me and shook my hand and that was it. Thought that was a bit cold of him, but then again, maybe he blamed me for splitting up the family or taking him away from his dad, I don't know but I felt a little bit of hostility there. Anyway, we all piled into a taxi bus and were soon on the way to his son's house. It was in a tiny out of the way place, in the middle of nowhere and it was bloody hot, so hot you had to gasp for air. Well, we arrived and we saw the house which was on stilts, complete with crawl space underneath. We were introduced to Steve's son's wife and little girl, shown where we would be sleeping and then whisked away just around the corner to meet Steve's first wife and new husband and more family. I could not believe what I was seeing here. We went straight into the back garden and a barbeque had been laid on for us and in the corner of the garden stood a Christmas tree. Yes! You heard right. A fucking Christmas tree, complete with decorations and lights. It was surreal. It was only November for Christ's sake but there it stood and then I had to check myself. It was coming up to Christmas and where we had left behind snow and ice, here, you could hardly breathe because of the heat which must have been around 30 degrees and also the humidity. Bloody hell, please, someone, give me a big fan that I could sit in front of. There were other kids there and the kids perked up a lot. Lots of food around, complete with flies everywhere, but the strangest thing was I felt myself being compelled to go sit with Steve's wife and talk to her. She was very nice and made me feel welcome and at ease. You have to remember that Steve was married to her long, long ago, long before he met me so I felt at ease with her and in the end we got on like a house on fire. Everyone was enjoying themselves but I needed to pee and asked if I could use the toilet. 'Yes,' someone said, 'it's over there,' and pointed me towards what looked like a wooden sentry box with a door. Oh shite!!! It was an outside DUNNY as they were called here. I opened the door very gingerly. I was told to lift up the seat before I used it in case there were spiders under the seat. I was in shock, because I had heard about the spiders in Australia, the black widow especially which was small, black and bloody deadly to humans. Why can't I just have a pee behind a bush when no one was looking???

I opened the door and saw there was a proper toilet, with a pull chain, but there was also a lot of bloody big cobwebs hanging from the roof of this basic wooden Dunny. I lifted the seat very carefully and it was clean and clear so I was safe for now. I must have had the quickest pee of my life, staring all around looking for things that had lots of legs and scuttled around my legs but it was okay and I could not wait to get out of there. I shot through the door like a bloody bullet. This was where Steve's wife lived, along with grandma. Can't believe it was a basic outside toilet which was like something out of the old ages. Well, had a quick pee, I'm sure the quickest pee in history and fled through the cobwebs to the outside sunshine again.

After that, we went back to the son's house and unpacked our things in the little spare bedroom. I was not impressed. His son had made up a make shift bed with no mattress and just consisted of solid boxes with wooden slats put over them. I was not impressed at all. The kids' beds were made up of beds on the floor and after what was supposed to be a good night's sleep, we were all totally fucked because everything was so uncomfortable. We didn't say anything but just didn't feel happy. Steve's son had a leaking fridge which was dropping to bits so Steve bought him a new one. His son had a freezer full of food but his dumb fridge was for beer only and that was the rule. Could not believe it. What a twat but it was his house and we could not say anything. None of us talked much and I thought his son was a bit of a bully. He treated his wife like shit and we never had deep conversations, not even father and son talks. It was very strange. Steve's son was dirty, never showered and was somewhat of a bully but he did introduce me to one thing, the local 4xxx beer which I started drinking a lot of.

I remember one day, climbing up a huge mango tree in his garden, absolutely pissed, barefooted and just in shorts and bikini top and climbed right to the top of the tree with my hand waving from the top branches, but I bloody suffered for that the next day as I became covered in bites from God knows what and ended up being put on antibiotics for a week. Won't do that again in a hurry. Just chilling in the garden one day, I thought it was extremely quiet and wondered where the kids were so went searching. Well, boy did I find them. Mike and Kelly were in the bedroom and mike had somehow got a pair of scissors and was sitting happily on the bed cutting off all of Kelly's long blonde hair. He had just about given her a crew cut, huge chunks were missing and her hair was almost shaved. Mike just thought it was all funny and I was enraged. I grabbed him and smacked him so hard on his arse that he took a long time to stop crying. *What a little fucker*, I thought to myself, thinking, there was the evil coming out in him again. I was in a panic and shouted for Steve and between us, we decided to take her to a little barber's shop in the middle of fucking nowhere, walking in the hot sun and asked the barber to shave her hair and I cried because I saw those blonde locks of hair disappear. I was enraged with Mike. He was evil personified and I ignored him and hated him for what he had done. Oh! And that was not the only thing he did. There was a massive garage room next to the house with a table to play table tennis on and although he seemed to like playing that game with his dad, he got it into his head one day to get hold of some matches and light a fire in the garage which he thought was great fun. It nearly burnt down and Steve's son was so angry because as it was the dry season, we could have got a $2,000 fine for that. What to do? What to do? I knew what to do, just keep drinking beer and remaining miserable and sad. Steve's son was never there and we left to just walk around to see the places near where we were living. There was a post office and believe it, a huge frilly lizard was basking on a stone outside. We never touched it but were told that he was the local resident that stayed on that stone in the sun all day. We also found a fish and chip shop and we ate Shark and chips. How bloody wonderful that tasted. One day we found a little park and sat on a seat and chatted while the kids had a run-around.

I spoke to hubby and told him I wasn't happy with being stuck in his son's house all day and had already found out there was a little town not far away called Ipswich and suggested that we take a taxi the next morning and go find a travel agent and find somewhere to go, just to be on our own for a while because coming here was not quite what we thought it would be like. Steve agreed so off we went in a taxi the next day. It was like a little shantytown. Basic, like something out of the movie Crocodile Dundee. I gazed at all the little shops and soon found a travel agent. I was the one that was independent with this and asked if there were any islands on the barrier reef that we could stay for a week's holiday. I was hooked on a little place called Hamilton Island on the reef itself.

It was expensive, had to fly out to it and there were no cars on the island at all. Well, we had the money and I just piped up with the words, 'Yes, that will do, can you book us for a week's stay, please? There were no problems and as we were a family, we would be first of all, staying in a little shack right near the sea for a couple of days, then were to be upgraded to a condominium. Oh! And we would be leaving in a couple of days. 'Yes,' I said straight away, 'let's go for it.'

We all needed a break, to be honest, from the monotony of being stuck in the house all day feeling bored and drinking beer. We all needed a change and I think this was just what was needed. It seemed that every day was boring and I felt so sorry for Kelly walking around with her crew-cut hair. She never complained but it broke my heart. Well, we got back to the house and told Steve's son and if looks could kill, I would be dead right now. I hadn't taken to like him at all and would be glad of the break, to be honest.

Well, two days later we were packed and gone. Steve's son wasn't anywhere to be seen but I didn't care. I was glad to get away from that house. If I remember rightly, it was only a couple of hours flying time and as we descended over a beautiful azure sea, the island came into view and then I nearly shit myself. It was tiny, between some high hills and the plane had to bank to come into the runway which was small and landed right at the edge of the sea. *Christ almighty*, I thought, *we are going to land in the sea*, because we were in a bloody big plane. That's when I was scared and felt sick but there was no need, the plane slammed on his brakes and made a perfect landing.

Stepping off that plane was magical. A little grass hut was the airport and we just walked through into an unreal, fantastic world. We were guided to our little thatched hut that was just big enough for all of us and it was wonderful. It was hot, there were palm trees everywhere and Kangaroos hopping all over the place and what we learned later were huge fruit bats hanging upside down in the trees until the dark when they spread their huge wings and flew away to feed. We were in paradise, a millionaire's paradise. There was a restaurant on the island and an Aussie pub with a balcony where you could get fantastic burgers. We went there every day. The next morning, we gazed out of our door and looked straight into the eyes of a kangaroo. It was all so surreal and rich. We all loved it and then we were told that we were moving up to a condominium which we would be better in because we were a family. I was fine with that and we were given directions and a golf cart to move our stuff. I will learn to drive this bleeding thing because it was just electric and there was just a push button to go and one to stop and a steering wheel. Could not go wrong with this because it was just two pedals and a steering wheel. I mastered it straight away and we drove up to our new apartment. It was great. Well, we moved into luxury. A massive apartment that had two bedrooms, a bathroom, living room and kitchen and a balcony that looked out onto a beautiful azure sea with white beaches. It was happiness itself.

We explored the island, Mike and Kelly found a huge big pool with dolphins in it and they would come up and let the kids stroke their heads.

One night, we all went to an outside barbeque where there were women dancing in hula skirts and Steve and myself had a lovely dance where the kids just looked on. It was a very rich island where I felt I could live forever but unfortunately, our holiday came to an end and we had to fly back to Brisbane. It was with heavy hearts that we had to go back to the mundane life at the house we were living in. The holiday was coming to an end. We went back to Brisbane and the house and the atmosphere was just doom and gloom. About a week before we flew back to England, just me, Steve and the kids found a wildlife park that was just a train ride away. Getting there was easy and we entered a magical land of koalas and kangaroos. We bought bags of food at the entrance to feed the kangaroos so we just walked around the park. I actually held a koala in my hands and had a photo of that taken. It pooed in my hands but it didn't bother me because I think it was nervous but what a great feeling that was to cuddle one of those. Then off we went to the kangaroos. There they were, all lying in a big field and I had the courage to sit down next to one. I stroked it and fed it some food and it gave me the most tremendous feeling at one with nature. Then, we decided to go see the emus. What a fucking big mistake that was. I approached them and had my hand full of food to feed them and one with big huge eyes just looked into my eyes and started to come towards me and then started to run faster towards me, in fact, I reckon it was running faster than I could, with its beady eyes on me. I finally got to the other side of the fence and it just crashed into it and came to a stop. Thank fuck for that.

Well, after that little expedition, we went back home, kids were laughing and my knees were shaking. *Oh well! It's an experience,* I thought to myself, *but not going there again.* Well, we were back at Steve's son's house and bored and really wanted to go home. Steve had sort of bonded with his kids but didn't really know them from being little so found it a bit uncomfortable and I think he wanted to go home as well.

One day just before we left, Steve's son woke me up very early one morning and told me to come outside the door. I was in my nightdress but half asleep, I just followed him down the stairs and into the street. He told me to look around at the wall of the house while me, standing in the road did so. All my life I have always been scared of spiders but never see one in Australia. It was as big as a dinner plate and Steve's son had a spade in his hand. In my life, I have never seen such a big thing. He smashed it with a spade and no! It did not die. This wasn't your regular little money spider, it was something you saw in horror movies. As he smashed, it fought hard, wrapping its big huge legs around the spade trying to fight for survival. I stood like a prat, in the middle of the road, in my nightie, screaming and begging for my life in case it got away and came for me. Eventually, it did die and was got rid of pronto because I refused to go back into the house until I didn't see it anymore. That was the icing on the fucking cake for me. I wanted to go home now, this minute but we were leaving in a few days anyway. Well, to be quite honest, I just wanted to leave and the day before we left, Steve and his son went for a walk and I got very pissed on the local beer but managed to pack our suitcases ready for the off.

Don't get me wrong, I loved the country, but apart from being on Hamilton Island, I hated where we were living, hated the way we were left on our own to find our own way around the place and as for me, there was no love lost with Steve's family at all. I had been looking after a little stray cat who had a grass seed lodged in her throat and found a vet who removed it and gave me some antibiotics, and she was cute and starting to get well but the day we were ready to leave, I asked Steve's son to carry on with the medication and make her better and he promised me he would, but later on, after we had left the country, I found out that he had smashed her little head in with a spade and killed her (he was very handy at using a spade, he was, the bastard). I always hated him after that and never forgave him.

The next day we went to the airport and trust me, there were not many tears shed. I just wanted to go home. On the flight going home, Mike wasn't sick and the kids behaved perfect and slept most of the way. We arrived back at our home and although it was winter and very cold, I think there was a sense of relief that we were back in our own home. Well, life returned to normal if that's what you called it. Steve parked his arse in his armchair and got fatter because he was living on chip shop food and choc ices and I looked after the kids. Same old same old. I did my best at being a mother but Mike soon got into his old ways of being a little bastard. It was soon time for him to move up to a big school, the last one and Kelly soon went behind.

Meanwhile, I had a tragedy of sorts. My periods were getting really heavy and I decided to go to the doctor who then sent me to hospital. It was discovered that I had something called Endometriosis, no idea what that was but was told I needed keyhole surgery for a complete hysterectomy. Okay! I could handle that.

I had to go into hospital for a couple of days then I came home. Well, I came home but was told by the doctors that they could not do a hysterectomy with the keyhole surgery and I would have to go back into hospital for a complete hysterectomy in a couple of weeks but they had to do proper surgery on me and cut everything out. Okay, I was okay with that too and was sent home. I remember after the keyhole crap that I felt okay for a couple of days but one day, I was lying on the sofa, watching telly with bleach on my hair and just resting and all of a sudden I felt the need to pee but when I sat on the toilet, all that came out was pure blood. Put a towel between my legs and got back on the sofa. What scared me was that the blood didn't stop gushing out of me. It soaked through the sofa and onto the floor and it was then I realised that it was not going to stop. I told Steve to phone an ambulance quickly. When they came in the door, they saw the bloodbath from the toilet to the sofa and onto the floor below. They put me on a stretcher and put me in the ambulance quickly. I was even dripping blood onto the ambulance floor. I didn't know what was happening but the ambulance men obviously did and blue lighted me to the hospital. All I remember after being taken to the hospital was being rushed to the operating room where I was cut wide open and everything was taken out and I also learned after that I had lost nearly all the blood in my body.

Chapter Nine
Early Menopause

I had to stay in hospital for a week, I was left with a huge scar right across the bottom of my stomach. I found out that I had four pints of blood pumped back into my body and then the consultant came to talk to me just before I was allowed home and informed me that as the surgeons had removed everything including my ovaries which produce hormones, I would probably go straight into the menopause, probably within the next three months and explained the symptoms I would begin to experience in my body. There would be hot flushes, mood swings, weight gain and vaginal dryness, but could not tell me how long these symptoms would last. *Bloody hell*, I thought to myself, *I'm only 43*. Menopause was only for old ladies probably in their late fifties or sixties.

That's me done then. I'm going to end up shrivelled and old and grey with a dry pussy. I went home feeling very sore because it was a massive scar across my stomach but also feeling very despondent about how I was going to feel and look in future months. Well, as I recovered, Steve had to walk more to help me look after the kids. He took them to their big school and fetched them back and as time passed, Mike got in with the wrong crowd at school, which made him worse within the family. He grew tall and started to bully all of us more and more. At thirteen, on his way home from school, he started drinking beer with his so-called mates and one time I watched him stagger home, falling over the fence into the garden and once inside, collapsed in a chair opposite the huge front window, and because he saw one of the schoolboys he hated, he did no more than find the nearest ornament and fling it at the window where Steve was sitting, so it smashed from inside the living room to the boy's face in the garden. Well, the whole window went out and yes! You guessed it, although the council came out and boarded it up, we had to pay for it because it was done by my drunken stupid son. Well, I had slowly recovered from my surgery so could move about okay but grew more despondent with each day that passed. Steve went back to his old ways of sitting by the window, watching his horse racing all day and putting on so much weight by wanting huge portions of crap food, even though I was a good cook and, in the end, he finally had to have a bed installed in the coner of the living room because he could not get up the stairs anymore because of the pain in his hip and he was still waiting to hear about his hip operation. Well, Mike was 13 years old, Kelly was 11 years old and I was really going through my menopause, the hot sweats, going through my body, my mood swings, my short temper, plus I had started drinking wine. I drank it with dinner, then just drank when I felt pressurised by anything. My son was out of control, didn't want to be seen walking down the street with me just because I wore clothes from second-hand shops and he felt ashamed of me. The compensation money from Steve's work had run out and we just lived on child benefit and disabled benefit from the social security. Kelly was eleven now and never ever complained and she was so close to me. Mike was stealing money from my purse which was food money, so one day I phoned the police, who arrived at our home and took him up to his bedroom for a good talk and he never did it again. (Stupid twat.) Will he ever grow up? Well, after that, I drank more and got more fed up. Steve slept downstairs, I started eating all my meals in the bedroom, then started watching television in the bedroom and really getting pissed off with all that was going on around me.

My mum was recovering from stomach cancer and I was due to go see her for her birthday as she was living in a warden aided bungalow in Nuthall, not far from Kimberley. The kids were at school and as I left, I knew what I was going to do, LEAVE! Again. Here I went again. I couldn't cope with Michael and could not carry out the demands of Steve so a couple of weeks before, I had hidden a bagful of clothes in a friend's bedsit, got myself a rented house a few streets away in Netherfield and walked out of that marriage as well. The only thing that broke my heart was that I had left yet another daughter behind and that broke my fucking heart as we were so close. My miracle baby who wasn't supposed to be born and was my little treasure. I had to question my actions that day and kept asking myself, why, oh why had I done it again? I couldn't stay still, I felt lost and had to keep moving but not knowing what I was looking for. The Gipsy coming out in me again, just like my real birth mother. The cow, I blamed her for everything that had happened to me. I was also trying to find something I had lost many years ago. The day of my mother's birthday I left home early, after the kids had gone to school, said goodbye to Steve and walked straight to my friend's house, picked up my hidden stash of clothes and instead of catching the bus to my mother's, walked into Netherfield and to the house I had rented. The landlord was waiting to hand me the door keys and in I went and locked myself away for the whole weekend, just thinking things over and trying to sort out what I was going to do next. I decided after the weekend to phone home and tell Steve I wanted to meet him on a park bench just up the road and that I needed to talk to him. Well, he turned up and so did the kids. Mike was coming up to fourteen then and Kelly was twelve. My heart wanted to burst from my chest with nerves but I knew I was going to be strong for myself and tell them everything. Well, I could tell that all their hearts were breaking and they asked me to come home but I firmly said NO and I was living in Netherfield, in a rented house, by myself. I also told them that I could not take any more of Mike's temper and threats and bullying, and the fact that no one lifted a finger in the house to help me, even Steve, who could walk with his crutches if he wanted to. They begged me to come back home but I said I was going to my new home and doubt it wouldn't take them long to find me. I turned to go to my house and they turned and walked away back home to theirs. It broke me yet again but I knew I had to be strong for myself but in another way, here I was, yet again, destroying my second family.

Well, I organised myself in the house but I also began drinking heavily. I suppose I thought that booze would take away the pain in my life but it didn't work because after sleeping it off, I felt like shit and just kept wanting more drink, to take the pain away of what I had done a second time. It also didn't take the kids long to find me because after a few weeks, there was a knock on the door and there stood my son Michael and Kelly. I think in the end, they spent more time in my house than in their real home. Well, I was happy there for now but my drinking got worse so I decided to go to my doctor and ask for help because I knew the way I was living was not healthy. He made an appointment for me to attend a day centre in town where I could get help getting off the alcohol. I would go twice a week and also be given drugs each day to wean me off the booze. My first appointment was for the next day, so while the kids stayed in my house just messing about, off I went, hoping to get the help I needed. After a check-up with the doctors and asking about my medical history, I was taken to a community room to meet people in the same boat as me. I was given two capsules to take and told to reduce my alcohol intake and come back two days later to have a check-up and two more capsules but, in the meantime, just mingle with the people there and talk about my problem. It was like a meeting room with a bunch of non-descript people just milling around talking about anything and everything. I felt awkward and sat alone most of the time until this glib fucking Irish man sauntered over and asked me my name and was I there for the same reason as the rest of them. He was good looking, smart with a smooth tongue and there I went again. I suppose it was out of loneliness more than anything but a lot of it was infatuation. I was so out of my safety zone at that time and vulnerable, I fell for his charms quickly. He asked if I would like to come to his flat which was just a bus ride away and I thought to myself, *Well, it is daytime and I won't stay long.* Also, thinking to myself more, *What the bloody hell am I doing? Am I not going through enough heartbreak already and I wasn't desperate for any man.* Well, being the stupid cow that I was, off I went, with Mr smooth-talking Irishman whose name was Alan and it didn't take us long to get to his flat which was on the ground floor and situated in St Ann's, in Nottingham. Never heard of the bloody place but went to his flat anyway. Well, his flat was on the ground floor and as I walked in, I noticed bare floorboards in the hallway, and as I turned into the living room, and looking into the kitchen, I noticed there was no bloody cooker. What the FUCK!!! Oh my God, what's going on here? He seemed proud of his little grotty flat and I felt drawn to him, but I don't know why. He put some music on, it was Irish and hideous and he opened a big bottle of cider and started drinking. What the bloody hell was he doing? We had just come from a meeting with other like-minded people, talking about our problems and given drugs to reduce our drinking and here he was, swigging straight from the bottle. I worked out that he was a serious drinker and didn't want the help that was out there. Well, he got drunk very quickly, decided he wanted to have sex with me and as I sat on the sofa, which I might add was really manky, decided to take off my panties. You have to remember that I was in my forties and should have known better, but I didn't and let him get on with it. He got as far as getting my panties off and was kneeling between my legs and then all of a sudden, he stopped and went very still and silent. I lifted my head and looked and there he was, stupefied and puke coming out of his mouth.

God, was I scared. He was just vomiting silently onto the carpet. I lifted my leg over his head and put my panties back on, put my coat on and high tailed it out of there and got the bus back to my rented home where my two kids were waiting. Well, it was all drugs and rock and roll going on when I got home. Dope smoking, everyone pissed. Well, I joined in for a bit but the next day, felt like shit and knew that in two days' time I had to be back at the clinic or meeting room for my next session of talking to like-minded people and getting my alcohol withdrawal drugs. Time passed quickly, and the kids went home to their dad every night which didn't feel right somehow but at that moment I was living in neverland with my life, but all that was about to change yet again. Off I went, two days later and there I was again, in the meeting room with the group and took my pills like a good girl and there he was "again". The Irish git came straight over and apologised and said he would like to try again, this time without the drink. Well, stupid muggins here fell for it again and after the meeting had finished, off I went on the bus to his flat. Looking around the flat, I didn't see any booze anywhere and he put that god awful Irish music on again, I really hated that crap and couldn't understand any of it. And another thing that made me surprised, he didn't want sex. Well, that's a first, but WAIT FOR IT! He looked me straight in the eye and asked me to move in with him! Oh, for fuck's sake, was he serious. He had no cooker, a chatty looking living room that looked like a doss house but I suddenly had a lightbulb moment. If I could get away from Netherfield, come live with this shitbag, then maybe I could get on the local council list and get myself a nice flat in St Ann's near Nottingham city centre and get right away from the house I was living in now and the kids would go back to living with their dad. You never know, luck may be on my side for a change, well it was, but not for long. 'Here we go again, Miss Longley,' my brain was saying, 'why the sodding hell could you not settle?'

Guess I was taking after my birth mother yet again, the wandering gipsy in me yet again. Thank you ma! I went back to the rented house, gathered all the clothes I had, a few other things and took off to St Ann's and moved in with the suave talking Irishman. The first thing I did was go to the local council and put my name down on the list and told them that I was being abused by an alcoholic and needed my own place as I was frightened of him (wasn't really but I wasn't going to tell them that). Although I did get the odd black eye when I was with him when he decided to swig from the bottle of cider but the only thing I couldn't get over was the fact that he just sat on the sofa and puked right onto the carpet. He disgusted me but I didn't clean him up, I just left him to it and when he sobered up, he just left his filth where it was and moved onto the next bit of carpet, dirty bastard. I stuck it out and kept hounding the council and they told me that I was at the top of the list and considered me a priority because of my circumstances with him. I slept in the same bed as him but when he was drunk, if I even went close to him, he would kick me viciously so I learnt to perch on the end of the bed to sleep.

I will always remember one day, I was so pissed off with him just sitting there drunk out of his skull that I wish he would die and then a thought came to my head. I was on automatic pilot and knew exactly what I wanted to do, KILL THE DRUNKEN BASTARD! I paced the living room floor and thought and thought and then I knew what I was going to do. I walked up to him, took the two-litre bottle of bloody cider from his hands, and he didn't know because he was out for the count, sitting up, just like a fucking statue. I went into the kitchen, took a whole packet of paracetamol and I took every tablet out of the packet, crushed it up in a bit of folded newspaper, and made into a powder and poured it back into the cider bottle, shook it a little, screwed the top back on and quietly slid it back between his hands and just sat there watching television. Well, eventually he woke up and carried on drinking, not even realising that I was there. I just kept giving sideward glances at him, hoping to God that something would take effect sooner rather than later. He finished the whole bottle, paracetamol and all, and he passed out again. I just left him where he was, sitting up, passed out and breathing. Shit, well that didn't work, did it? Because a short time later, he woke up and asked me to go down to the shop and buy him some more drinks.

I decided to move him in with me but only if he stopped drinking and went to his doctor and got involved in AA meetings and he agreed. In fact, I took him to the bloody doctors to make sure he got the help he needed. Well, with that setup, I went back to the rented house in Netherfield and collected the few things that belonged to me and just took off to St Ann's which was almost in the city of Nottingham with a good chance of getting my own flat. I got involved with the local church and asked the vicar if he knew Alan, and he certainly did. He also advised me that although when sober, Alan did sometimes go to this church, mainly for handouts, not to get involved with him because he was the local drunk and nasty when pissed, but I told him that I was or had moved in with him and could he help him to have a cooker installed as I had no money for one and Alan certainly didn't. He told me to be very careful but didn't say any more. Well, I moved in and sorted the flat out. Pisshead had got his medication from the doctors and I made sure he took them and started to go to AA meetings as well. All was good for quite a while. I also found that he was a fantastic guitar player. He seemed to have calmed down and was quite a pleasant man when sober and

I already had my plan in place about getting my own place. I decided to scout the papers for a local cleaning job to make up my money because he wasn't working and I needed a bit of extra cash. Well, I found myself a little part-time cleaning job in the paper and after speaking on the phone to the boss, was told I could start straight away. I would get a phone call, with an address to go and clean up. I was okay with that, I thought to myself but one thing bothered me. The prat I was living with would be on his own, with his thoughts and his addiction but was quite happy for me to go to work. He promised me he would be fine and I trusted his word.

In the meantime, my Kelly had found out where I lived and turned up one night while I was asleep. There was a little knock on the door and there she stood, only to tell me that the little cat named Lappy who we had since a kitten, had died of cancer. She was old, but my daughter was in tears. She could not stay as she had a taxi waiting but her parting words to me were, 'Oh! Mum, Mike says he never wants to speak to you again,' and with that, she was gone, back to her dad's. You may have thought I was gobsmacked, but nothing was further from my mind.

'Well, sod him, the little shit,' or maybe not so little now as he had reached the age of seventeen and Kelly was fifteen. As I carried on working, things were not too bad and one day I got the phone call I had been waiting for. The council had found me a flat just down the road from where I lived now and asked if I would like to have a look. I jumped at the chance and one day, when I was not working, I picked up the keys from the local council office and went to have a look. Well, the first look was not looking good. The front window had been smashed in and no one had lived there for a very long time. I opened the door and walked in with trepidation. I was quite surprised, although it stank of dead things, finding out later that the man who had lived there before had kept lots of cats and as they died, he had just left them to rot or mummify. He must have been a hoarder. Apart from that, it had been painted and cleaned. There were two bedrooms, a bathroom, a separate toilet and a nice kitchen and a huge living room. I took it straight away and as I was earning I arranged to have the whole place carpeted, and furnished and the church gave me a lovely dining room table with six chairs and also a beautiful new huge sofa and two armchairs and I bought a bed and wardrobe. The Vicar of the church warned me once again to not let Alan live with me. I said okay, knowing that the lease was in my single name only. I was such a stupid cow because when I walked back to his flat which was

111

only over the road, went indoors and there he was, pissed as a fart, swigging on a two-litre bottle of cheap cider and trying to talk but couldn't because he was so drunk. *Here we go again*, I thought to myself and where he got the drink from I have no idea but once a drunk, always a drunk. I gathered my few things and walked out the door, telling him I was going to my new flat and I did just that. It felt lovely, sitting there in my new home and I had made it look lovely. I carried on working and earning but after about a week, I couldn't resist going up to see Alan. Yes, I know people "MUGGINS" again. Anyway, I went up and just walked straight in and there he was, fast asleep on the sofa, yet another bottle of cider empty beside him. I still felt sorry for him and shook him awake and told him I was going to pack his things and take him down to my new flat. He mumbled a bit but finally, I took him to where he was going to live with me, but I never put his name on my tenancy agreement. I wasn't that stupid, but putting him in my home was, as I was soon to find out, the worst thing I ever did.

He didn't drink all the time and as I was working part-time, I could keep my eye on him. At that time, I decided to buy myself a computer and have the internet installed. He was happy with that because he could involve himself in video games online which hopefully it did. I also, in my time off, created a website about my life in which I learnt how to do so many things and made so many things. Life went on and Kelly came over a few times but Mike stayed away and he didn't see me for three whole years and I also found out that he had been spreading rumours about me trying to kill him whilst he was still in my womb! What the fuck! After all the hardship and surgery I went through to get pregnant with him, I was told he was down the pub telling all his mates that's what I did and he still does to this day. What an evil person he was. That's why he never loved me and always hated being with me and that's why he was and still is never close. Well, fuck him, the turd. I think he ought to have gone to anger management classes because his brain was arse about-faced. Well, enough of that.

Our life went on but as time went on, when he was drinking, I occasionally went to work with a black eye where he had smacked me for no reason, but I still carried on, hoping I could make him better but thinking about the warning that the Vicar from his church had given me. With his playing on his computer games, he stopped drinking for a while and seemed nice for a change. Then another shock was about to enter my life. I actually had a call from Mike, my son who told me Kelly had been rushed to the hospital and had to have emergency surgery. I told Alan, I rushed to the hospital and found out that my beloved daughter who was fifteen was going down for emergency surgery because she had a baby growing in her fallopian tube and could die if they didn't operate. I rushed to her side and found her very ill. Apparently, she had collapsed at her dad's house and got rushed to hospital. She was fifteen and gotten pregnant and didn't know and the baby was dead in one of her fallopian tubes. She would die without surgery. I sat with her for a bit and could tell she was very scared. As the doctors came to take her to surgery, my son asked me if I was going to wait and unbelievably said NO, I was going home and he just looked at me in disgust. I could not blame him and he looked at me in disgust as I left. I should have stayed but something was pulling me back to St Ann's because I had to keep my eyes on the drunk. What sort of mother does that to her child? I felt like an evil witch but left anyway. There I go again, something in my brain telling me that I wanted to walk away from any situation that was put in front of me. I don't know whether it was because I had been groomed from way before, when I was a teenager myself and could not handle anything, I just don't know but I left the hospital, got a taxi and went back to St Ann's.

I found the boyfriend passed out on my sofa. I was so fucking angry that I stood over him and started smacking him across the face time after time until he woke up. He suddenly came to and I kept smacking him and calling him a drunken bastard and as fast as lightning, he sat up and punched me in the face, giving me a black eye. After he had come around properly, he couldn't do enough for me and was full of apologies and kept saying he was sorry and he would never do it again. *Oh, where had I heard that before?* London and that gangster prick came to mind. Well, I kept in touch with the hospital and Kelly was recovering and would soon be able to go home where her dad could keep an eye on her. I had to carry on working and Alan spent nearly every day playing games on his computer which was good because it kept him away from the bottle for a while.

By now, Mike was seventeen and was working and Kelly, after her recovery had reached sixteen and started visiting me every so often. Things were running smoothly for a change. Sir stayed sober for quite some time so I decided to get married to the guy. I bought a wedding dress from a second-hand shop with a veil, fixed a date, made my own buffet in my flat and paid for a Rolls Royce to the registry office. (My mistakes were huge and I have no reason for the things I did.) I also ordered a huge number of bottled wines and made fuck face promise not to touch them. He promised and I took him at his word, (me, silly cow!). I had invited all the girls and the boss to this wedding. Not my kids because they didn't know anything about it. And so it goes, another wedding. What the bloody hell was I thinking, but I was about to find out later.

Chapter Ten

An Experience with Chat Rooms

All the wedding guests went home happy and drunk and I had another husband. Husband number three. What was I thinking? I knew deep in my heart that I didn't love him, I think I just wanted someone to keep me company. Must admit though, all through the reception in my living room, Alan was the only one who stayed sober. As soon as the last guest left, he turned to me and said, 'Now it's my turn,' and took an opened bottle of wine and started guzzling. Oh, God! I had been trying so very hard to keep him away from the drink and thought I was doing pretty good until now. Didn't argue with him, there were too many bottles around and I didn't want to get hurt so just started to clear away the food and clean up and get on with it. What a bastard! He had let me down again. I thought to myself, and this fuckin stupid marriage was not going to last because I was not prepared to get used as a punch bag again. I kept quiet, waited until he passed out and then took all the wine bottles away and crept outside to the shed and put everyone in there and closed and locked the door. I went to bed but slept lightly because I just didn't know what to expect. Got through the night, all was quiet and I had to get ready for work. Yes! That's right, life went on as normal. There was no honeymoon, and there was no engagement ring actually. Eventually, I had four husbands and there was only one who put an engagement ring on my finger when I was sixteen and that was my first love, and I felt so proud wearing it but have never had one since. Anyway, worked all day at different places and when I got back home, Sir had sobered up and was waiting for me. He had a mean look on his face and asked where all the wine had gone. Well, I couldn't tell him I had poured it all down the sink, could I? Or he would have kicked the shit out of me so I told him it was in the shed. He got the key from the kitchen and went to the shed and must have carried about ten full bottles of wine back and put them in the kitchen. He started drinking them straight away and I don't think he even realised he had a new wife. I was already working my arse off and earned most of the money that came into the flat, and at that time, it was cash in hand with every job I completed. Must admit though, I did enjoy the people I worked for and I got on well with them. Well, Kelly popped in every so often. She was sixteen now and had a new boyfriend. Mike stayed away and as I mentioned did not see or talk to me for three years. I think that was because I had left his dad, he hated me for that. Oh! And the fact that he kept telling everyone that I had tried to kill him while he was growing in my stomach. Don't know how that one worked out because when the time came for him to come out, he didn't want to. He seemed to like where he was, stubborn little git.

Anyway, back to my marriage of sorts. He carried on drinking and I carried on working, and occasionally, when he had his sober moments, he was on the computer, playing war games or violent ones and stayed in the spare bedroom most of the day. Suited me down to the ground but one day, I came home from work and found him very drunk, still standing and in the kitchen. As I stood at the kitchen door, I asked him what was wrong and with the most evil look on his face, he turned and came at me out of the blue and put his hands around my neck and started squeezing so tight that I couldn't even cry for help or breath and it was at this time that Kelly popped through the front door to see me and found me semiconscious on the floor because seeing her shocked him into letting go of my throat. Well, she went for him with a fury like I had never known and beat the living crap out of him and he didn't fight back and warned him that if he ever hurt me again, she would fuckin kill him. I think that sobered him up quite quickly as she helped me up from the floor and into a chair.

She was very reluctant to leave me alone with him but I told her I would be fine and get him sorted the next day. While he was still sleeping it off and I had one of my days off, I went to the local community centre to see the boss and asked him if there were any little programmes that prick face could get involved in, (I did mention him by his real name, don't worry.). I was in luck! Or rather Alan would be. In the workshops there they had a computer room with lots of computers dotted around the room and youngsters could go there and learn how to work them and programme them. The boss told me to ask Alan to come down and if he was okay, then he could start straight away. *Perfect, just bloody perfect,* I thought. I walked straight back to my flat, shook him awake and told him to have a shave and get his act together as I had got him a little job.

He was not very happy about that but as he was not able to remember what he had done to me the night before when he looked at the finger mark bruises around my neck, he went very quiet and agreed to go with me to St Ann's Square to see the man he would be working with on the computers. Well, things went very well for a year or more and he never drank during that time and I also made sure that there was no alcohol in the house whatsoever and poured what I found hidden down the sink. I worked hard and for once, began to trust him until on one of the days I had off, I received a phone call from the community centre asking if Alan was at home as he wasn't there. *Oh! For fuck's sake,* I thought to myself, *not again.* My heart dropped to the floor as there could only be one explanation. I told the centre that I would have a walk around the streets as he wasn't at home and I hadn't seen him. Well, I started traipsing around the streets and also all the little alleys that honeycombed the area and was a favourite place for drug takers and drug dealers. *Good job, its daylight,* I thought to myself as no one in their right mind would walk around here at night. Well, surprise surprise, I walked around a corner to find Alan and another scruffy-looking man bending over a young girl. Alan was drunk, but not that drunk and as I got closer I saw him trying to inject this young drug-addicted girl with a hypodermic syringe full of God knows what into her arm. He turned when he saw me but because his reflexes were slower than mine, he could not catch me when I turned and ran. I ran as fast as I could up and down the little walkways and got home, locked the door and put the dead bolts on both doors to the locked position. That was it. I had finally had enough and it was a mere few seconds before his face was at the window and he was begging to be let in and in the background was the little scruffy scrote that he had been with.

This time, I phoned the police who turned up quick time. I kept the bloody door locked all this time until one of the policemen came and knocked and asked if he could talk to me. I let him in but asked that Alan stayed outside, even though he told the coppers that he was my husband and lived there. I explained to the policeman what I had caught him doing with the young girl, also that he was an alcoholic and I had been abused a lot. I also showed him my tenancy agreement, which only had my maiden name on it and that I didn't want him in the flat anymore as I was frightened of him. He told me he understood and asked me to put a few clothes in a bag for Alan and they would take him away to the council, where hopefully, he would be re-homed. I ran to the bedroom and put some bits of underwear and a couple of shirts in a carrier bag and handed them to the police.

I begged them not to let him come near the flat again and they promised it would be sorted. With that, I saw the police take him away and that was that. I would never see him again, thank God. I gave up my work completely and set about finding a solicitor that would come to my home and start divorce proceedings and a lovely lady turned up and sorted everything for me. I didn't have to go to court and because of the domestic abuse I had suffered. It went through quite quickly and I received my divorce through the post via the court. I could not have been happier. Well, after getting rid of the drunken prick, I enjoyed the peace and quiet, got myself a couple of cats and lived on benefits.

After about a year, I had built my own personal website which was really cool for me because I had to learn a lot but made lots of friends online. Then I started getting bored, so I experimented with the MSN chat rooms, really for a bit of fun at first. It was quite interesting at first, meeting people and I enjoyed myself talking to people, but one day I had a visit from Steve, Kelly's dad. He got my address from Kelly, knocked and came straight in. We still got on well even though we no longer lived together. He told me to sit down as he had something to tell me.

'Oh god! What have I done now!'

He looked me straight in the eyes and told me that my mother had died three years earlier but the kids were afraid to tell me because my mother had said to them on her death bed that if they ever mentioned her, then she would come back and haunt them. She never forgave me for leaving their dad and what she said to them scared them shitless, so they never told me for all those years. I went numb, couldn't even shed any tears because I never thought she loved me when I was a little girl and when I turned rebellious, loved me even less, and when I got pregnant, I think she was just disgusted with me and ashamed of me so we were never close after that. Don't get me wrong, I knew she had cancer and was even with her when the doctors told her and was at her bedside when they removed a tumour from her stomach weighing about two stone, but after she came home from the hospital and got her strength back, it was around that time that I left Steve and she told him she never wanted to speak to me again. No love lost there then and I suppose that's why I didn't cry. I was just very quiet and asked Steve where she was buried. He told me Kimberley Cemetery, with my dad. I made myself a promise that I would go and pay my respects one day, but it wasn't until 2009 that I made that trip. Steve left after a little while and I just remained quiet and went back on my computer. I promised myself that I would go and put some

118

flowers on my mum and dad's grave at some point but at that moment in time, I just messed about on the computer, building on my website, (which is no more, I'm afraid), then decided to go on MSN to see what was going on.

Well, I was mildly surprised to find that there were a couple of blokes online. I started talking to a bloke that lived in Lichfield, Staffordshire. We got friendly and to my surprise, I found out that he was middle-aged, like me. Had been divorced for ages and lived alone in a three-bedroomed house which sounded posh to me. We talked a lot for weeks and I found out that he lived near Cannock Chase and loved walking and hiking. Wasn't that "The Cannock Chase" where years ago, the bodies of girls had been buried??? He sent me a photo and then asked me to go stay with him for a weekend.

Bloody hell! That was quick. Surely it could not do any harm and so I arranged to let Kelly feed my cats, all three of them. Yes, I love animals, sometimes they are more comfort than people. So, off I went on this wild stupid journey to meet a man I didn't really know. (Could have been a fuckin axe murderer for all I knew.) Sometimes throughout my life I have been impulsive and this journey was to be just that. I had to get a train from Nottingham to Birmingham, then change and get the Lichfield train and he would meet me at the station. I was going to stay from Saturday until Monday, so it wasn't that long and I could always make a run for it and get the next train back, couldn't I? If I didn't like what I saw.

Well, I made that journey and did like what I saw. He wasn't much to look at but was slightly shy and talked a bit posh and had a car. Well, we shook hands, yes, that's right, and he was the proper gentleman. I didn't talk much but took in the beautiful countryside as we drove to his house. To be quite honest, I was looking for "woods", thick dense woods, Cannock Chase, to be quite honest. Hope he wasn't going to drive me there, do bad things to me, then bury me. Wonder if he had a spade in the boot of his car??? Oh well, nothing worse can happen, can it? So let's go for it.

I needn't have worried, we drove into this little village and pulled up outside a lovely detached house which was where he lived. He turned and said he would cook me some dinner and then we could go for a walk around Cannock Chase and he would show me the countryside. *Oh shit*, thinking to myself, *it was always the quiet unassuming men that turned out to be serial killers.* My heart was racing but I took my overnight bag from the back seat and he walked me to the door. Well, it was posh. There was a little hallway where you wiped your feet, then another hallway where the phone table was then straight into the living room. *Very nice*, I thought, gazing out through the sliding glass doors onto a superbly manicured lawn. It was huge. D told me to bring my bag and he said I could choose a bedroom. Well, it wasn't going to be his that's for sure, so I chose the smallest one with a television and said I would stay there. He seemed happy with that and went downstairs to make dinner for us.

Well, let's just wait and see, I thought. He said we were going for a walk and hoped I had a good pair of trainers, as he was going to show me around where he lived. *Okay!* I thought, I can handle that but stayed quiet but curious. Well, after lunch we did go for that walk and to be honest, I was knackered and yes, he did take me all the way around Cannock Chase, up-hill, and down dale and to be quite honest, I just wanted to go back to his and clean up and have a rest. Back at his, we sat on the sofa and I told him about my life, that I had kids and had just moved in a while ago to a new flat and he told me that his wife of many years had left him for another man, he divorced her and she went on to have twins with this other guy. He worked at some company or other and we just sat there watching television and chilling. Later on, he took me to his local pub for a drink and a meal, but to be honest, all I wanted to do was go back to his and sleep. He was quite boring, to be honest, and I just wanted to go to bed. I ran a bath, put on some pyjamas and went to my room. He looked at me with hope in his eyes and I thought, *No way mate, I'm going to bed,* and with that, I went to the little bedroom and closed the door and slept like a baby. It was so quiet in the countryside and I was definitely not used to it, but it was nice.

The next morning, I woke up refreshed, had a wash and went downstairs and found D had cooked me breakfast. We did a lot of bloody walking again that day as well. He showed me around all the shops in Litchfield, plus the cathedral, which I must add, was quite stunning then we went back to his for a restful afternoon watching television. I had to keep going into the garden for a smoke, which he disapproved of immensely. He hated that I was a smoker so I spent most of the afternoon sitting in the garden. He was quite the snob really and I had to sit and watch most of the programmes he liked which were quite boring really. We had dinner. I cooked spaghetti Bolognese which he ate but don't think he liked it very much. I kept looking at him, trying to weigh him up. I thought he was a snob, loved himself, kept everything in order and had a very strict routine about everything. If I were to say out loud what I really thought about him, he was up his own arse, to be honest. The night drew in and I was due to go home the next day and I knew what he wanted that night so when it was time for bed, I went for a bath, put on a little short nightdress and went into the bedroom and sat on the end of his bed. I really didn't want this but thought, *Well, let's get it over with.*

He sat next to me on the bed and started kissing me and he had such bad breath I nearly gagged but just let him carry on. We both lay on his bed and the inevitable happened but it wasn't the passion and the WOW factor I had been waiting for, it was on top, thank you, ma'am, while I just stared at the ceiling and thought of Nottingham, to be honest, and getting back home. There was no groaning, no yelling with passion, there was nothing. It was all so quiet, you could have heard a bloody pin drop. Well, he climbed off me and turned over and went to sleep, and so did I. Thank God, I was going back home the next day. Well, he asked if he could see me again and after a little consideration, I thought to myself, *well, yes he can see me again but he must come and stay at my flat.* He agreed to that and I said I would be in touch with him when I got home.

Once on the train, I felt at ease and could not wait to get back to my home, my cats and Kelly. Once home, I cleaned everywhere and felt happy again. No drunken arsehole banging on my door. God knows where he lived now and didn't care. Kelly was with her boyfriend in his home, Mike had got his own flat not far from me and had got a girlfriend who was soon to become his wife. His second wife as it happens, he had divorced his first wife, or rather she divorced him due to his unruly behaviour, but they had a little boy who I did babysit for a couple of times. I was now a grandma and proud of it and he has grown into a fine young man with a girlfriend and a house of his own where they live together and he has a good job as an engineer.

Anyway, back to my blind date. Yes, I did invite him up for a couple of visits and introduced him to my daughter and my cats. For the next two years began an adventure, sadness, heartbreak, dominance and overall stupidity on my part AGAIN! Why can't I ever be content and happy? Pisses me right off, that does. He came over one weekend and I told him I had arranged a special party for my daughter who was going to be 21. I had ordered an Elvis Presley look-alike show for her in the local pub and got dressed up and off we went. Everything went fantastic and when she arrived, everything was set up and on time, in she walked. My God, she did look stunning with her long blonde hair and beautiful dress and perfect make-up. I presented her with a huge bouquet of flowers and she was absolutely gobsmacked when "Elvis" started singing.

Everything went just perfect and she even got up on stage with this handsome man and sang with him and it was wonderful to see her so happy. It was when I took bossy boots back to the flat that he suddenly turned to me and asked me if I would like to go and live with him in his house in Litchfield. What! He wanted me to leave behind all my furniture and just take my clothes and my cats. Christ! He had no idea what he was letting himself in for. Kelly didn't want me to go because we were very close at that time and I would be too far away from her but in this case, my stupid head ruled my heart and I said yes to him. I would be living in a lovely house with a garden for the cats, who had been indoor cats while in the flat. The next weekend, he came up to my place and I packed everything up and put three cats on the back seat of his car in baskets and gave the door keys to my neighbour and off we went. Maybe I was in for a better life, you never know (who the fuck was I kidding). Well, arrived safely, put the cat litter tray in an alcove off the kitchen, got my clothes and stuff and put all of them in the wardrobe in the small bedroom that I slept in the first night and then, introduced the cats to the huge garden out back. Little did I know that they were to be left outside all the time and the smallest cat was a Devon Rex.

A Devon Rex has no fur and I was angry with Mr Snob for suggesting any of them stayed outside. I demanded that they be let out for a little while when it was sunny, but most times they were to come and go as they pleased. I had a little Persian cat named Ayeesha, a huge mixed breed cat named Foo, and my little Devon Rex who I named Batman because of his huge ears. I think that was the first obstacle I had to put straight with this man. I was not going to live by all of his rules, I made some too. Well, we chugged along for a while, and I got a good cleaning job in the area cleaning Posh people's houses and mansions. I was trustworthy and well-liked and enjoyed my job immensely. Mr Snob ended up being put on three days a week at his job because they were laying people off, I never found out what he did and I didn't care to be honest. I managed to make three trips to Mount Snowdon and climbed it three times, and never took the train up to the top once. D took me to a lot of places to climb and hike and I must admit I did enjoy the freedom it gave me. When I wasn't climbing, I was working and of course, I had to contribute part of my earnings to the upkeep of the house. My only beef with this man at that time was the disagreements we had over my cats. My heart was breaking because I had three cats who were used to being in the warmth of a flat to sleeping outside and fending for themselves. The only one that was allowed to stay in at night was Batman because he had no fur to keep his little body warm. The other two stayed out and I even had to put their food outside in the end.

This went on for some time until I decided one day to put an advert in the paper for someone with a family to adopt Ayeesha because she was a tiny Persian who was frail because she was made to stay outside in all weathers. A family came to see her and after I gave her a cuddle, I handed her over and this family promised to take good care of her and off she went. That left just Foo and Batman. Foo was a huge ginger tomcat who was like a lion and my son decided he would like to have him. Well, the control freak decided to take me to my son's house back in Nottingham, and I had Foo in his basket on the back seat of the car. Didn't take long to get to his house where he lived with his second wife and indoors we went. Well, it was a bloody fiasco as anyone knows that if you move a cat into a new house, you have to keep them indoors for a couple of weeks so that they can get used to their surroundings. Oh no! Not my son, the stupid idiot. He decided to tie a bit of string around his neck and use it as a lead to take my cat outside into the garden. Foo was a huge ginger tomcat and once outside, he was so scared, he took off at lightning speed and ended up on someone's garage roof. Well, that was that. He would not come off the roof, terrified by his surroundings, and simply vanished. Well, that did it for me. I was angry beyond words and told bossy arse to fuck off home as I was going to stay at my son's house for a couple of days, sleeping in the spare bedroom and scouring the streets looking for my cat. Told bossy arse to come back after two days and pick me up. The absolute stupidity of what my son had done was beyond belief and for the next two days and nights, I spent hours, walking the streets with a box of crunchies, calling his name, but to no avail. It made me heartbroken and my mind was made up for when I got back to Lichfield, knowing that my loving cat was out there somewhere, Lost, looking for me, maybe even being run over. I made it clear to my son what a stupid thoughtless twat he was and when I didn't find my cat, D came to take me back home, but it wouldn't be for long, I can assure you. I had already made up my mind, I was coming back to Nottingham when I had made a plan. Still heartbroken about my cat and my stupid son, I went back to working and he went back to his job. I became more pissed off with each day that passed but a bigger bombshell was about to hit. It was early morning and the house phone was ringing, around 5 am. I went to answer it and my son on the other end told me that their dad had just had a heart attack and was in hospital in Nottingham. He told me to get to the hospital straight away as it was serious.

Apparently, their dad had felt strange and phoned my son in the middle of the night asking him to come over. When my son got there, he saw the state of his dad and phoned for an ambulance straight away. The paramedics came almost immediately and my son told me that as the paramedics were taking him along the garden path, his dad had collapsed and his heart had stopped beating. The ambulance men managed to get his heart started and once in the ambulance, blue-lighted him straight to the hospital. 'Mum! You have to come now.'

'Okay, calm down,' I replied and put the phone down. I went upstairs and believe it or not the stuck-up bastard was still asleep. I damn well shook him awake and told him to get dressed and get me to the hospital in Nottingham NOW!!!

I explained that the kid's dad had had a heart attack and had been rushed to hospital and I needed to be there with them. I got dressed and told him to get the car ready. He did as I asked but I could tell he wasn't happy. *Sod him*, I thought to myself, about time he got his finger out of his arse and did something for me for a change. I was tired and worried and just wanted him to put his foot down and get me there. Arriving at the hospital, I found the heart ward and gave my name, and was taken there with D trailing behind me. When I arrived, I found my daughter walking up and down the ward crying and not coping, and my son just sitting outside the ward in shock, waiting for me. I told the doctors who were working on Steve and they allowed me to go in and see him. As I entered this important ward, I saw my kid's dad wired up to machines and stickers all over his chest and he was conscious and recognised me straight away. I went up to his bedside and the look of fear in his eyes told me just how scared he was. I hugged him and all he kept telling me was, 'Please don't let me die.'

I was crying and promised him everything would be okay, but I didn't know, I just said that to calm him down. The consultant told me that he was going to keep him in for a few days until he was stabilised and with that, I said my goodbyes and went to my children. They were very upset so I made the decision to stay at our family home for a few days until he was well enough to come home. I turned to Mr uppity and told him I was going to stay at my old home where the kids had grown up and that I would phone him when I wanted to come back so he could come and fetch me. He looked a bit downtrodden at that moment, but family came first and I was staying put, so off he went, all the way back to Lichfield.

Well, Mike took us back to where we used to live and as he had a home and a wife, and Kelly was living with her boyfriend, I was given the keys and was dropped off at the house the children grew up in. It seemed strange going back into that house after such a long time but decided to make the best of it for the next few days. I went up to the large bedroom and found it looking like a bomb had hit it. Kelly had been staying at the house until she met her boyfriend and the room was disgusting. There were plates of mouldy food and clothes everywhere. I was too tired that day to be bothered about cleaning up and just fell into her bed, exhausted both mentally and physically. I stayed at the house, visiting Steve once as he was improving and was going to be coming home soon. When that happened, Mike could pop over every day and make sure he was okay. I cleaned the house up and then phoned sir to come and fetch me as I had to get back to work.

Well from then on things went from bad to worse. I became very unhappy with my situation. I did not love this man I was with. I think I was in love with the whole idea of living in a nice home in a posh area and the travel that went with it. (Who was I bloody kidding?) One day I made up my mind to leave, just like that. I wasn't working that day but he was so I packed my clothes and my toothbrush into a black bag liner, phoned a taxi driver I knew in Nottingham to come fetch me and gave him the address. He said he would be there in around two hours and I just sat and waited.

The hardest decision I've ever had to make was leaving my one and only little cat Batman behind. He was happy where he was and sir loved him and let him stay indoors with him, so he was used to the house, so when the taxi arrived, with a heart that was broken yet again over leaving my cat, I bundled everything into the back seat and as I left, I turned to see my little cat walking onto the front lawn and just sitting there looking at me. I knew I had deserted him. I loved him so much that I cried tears until I had no more left in me. Putting on a brave face, I began to feel better as we got closer to Nottingham and my daughter's bedroom, not knowing that she had already left her first boyfriend because of domestic drunken violent abuse she had suffered at the hands of him. I felt instant relief when I arrived and took my bag of belongings straight upstairs, only to find Kelly was back in the bedroom also with her cat, a little female Devon Rex cat called MooMoo. Also while I had been back in Lichfield after her dad's heart attack, he had also had a hip replacement and lost a lot of weight which helped him to recover much more quickly. Well, I stayed there for a while, living day by day and also decided to go see my local council to tell them I was living in my daughter's bedroom and could they find me a flat for someone over fifty. It wasn't long before I got a phone call to go and look at a flat in Carlton, just up the road, I saw it and said yes and that was that. It was warden aided and was on the second floor of a four-story block. Well, I went to town on that one bedroomed flat. I got myself a credit card, and I furnished it out completely because when I went to see it, it was nothing but bare floorboards and empty.

For a few days, I slept on the floor in the living room, in a sleeping bag. I ate at the Chinese restaurant up the road until the carpets were laid, I went out to buy furniture, and eventually, I made the flat look beautiful. I hung pictures on the wall and made myself at home. Kelly came to see me often and asked if I could enquire about her dad getting a flat in the same block. Well, I did my best and after a while, I had a reply telling me that he qualified for a one-bedroom flat on the ground floor because he was disabled. Well, that was good and I did not mind that he would be living two floors down because although we were not together anymore, we still remained friends. I left all the moving to my son because he had a van and could do it and finally he was living comfortably below me and we were always in each other's flat. Kelly came to see us a lot, and at that time, there was a fruit and veg man who came in a van to deliver fresh fruit and veg to the old people in the complex. Well, need I say more, he was handsome and young and virile and Kelly had started to get to know him and fancied him like mad. His name was Joe and there was a certain chemistry between them. I just left them to it and eventually, they had rented a flat just down the road from me and before I knew it, Kelly was pregnant with his baby. 'Oh shit.' She hardly knew him, she only had one fallopian tube. Please God, tell me this isn't happening. Kelly was absolutely smitten with him and he continued to come selling his fruit and veg and having a relationship with my daughter. I could not step in because she was old enough to make up her own mind.

Well, things happened quickly after that. Kelly realised that Joe took drugs, the hard stuff, Cocaine, and many times when I went down to see her, I found Joe passed out on the living room floor, but she was besotted with him and I could not say anything. I think finally the penny dropped and she moved out and went to live in a friend's spare room in a house on Conway road. I think she realised how dangerous it all was and just vanished out of his life. Well, as she started getting bigger, she moved yet again and found a grotty flat just behind the block where I and her dad was living. She was very close to her dad and it seemed appropriate that she was so close to him.

One day as I was in Steve's flat, he had noticed a lump sticking out of his throat and couldn't swallow properly so Kelly decided to go with him to his doctor's where he was sent off to hospital and had a scan on his throat. Another bombshell, he was diagnosed with throat cancer and had to start radiotherapy immediately. (Will it ever fucking end?)

Story of my life, more downers than uppers. Am I ever going to find happiness?

Well he started therapy but didn't get any better and although Kelly kept an eye on him, he began to get poorly but he still kept going over the road to the bookies and having a fling on the horses, bless him. It was around this time that although I was settled in my flat, I had a phone call from Kelly one night. She was in a pub in Netherfield, just down the road and asked me to go down and keep her company. When I arrived, she was there, sitting at a table drinking coffee and doing a crossword, so I went to sit with her to keep her company. She was alone now and I thought she needed time with her mum. That part was alright but it was the last biggest mistake of my bloody life. (Oh god, will I ever learn? Obviously not!)

Chapter Eleven
A Birth, A Death and A Near-Death Experience

I popped down to see Kelly and as we sat talking. This handsome middle-aged man came over to talk to Kelly. He was telling her that the tattoo of the Rolling Stones on her arm was the wrong way 'round. Obviously, he was a great fan of the group. Don't tell me he was chatting her up for god's sake, he was old enough to be her father. She introduced me as her mum and as soon as he heard that, he moved his chair around and sat next to me. Kelly looked a bit pissed off with him because she just wanted it to be me and her for a couple of hours. He was good looking, I must admit. He was tall, had a shock of grey hair and was dressed quite smart and seemed quite interested in me because he said he liked older women. I looked at Kelly, she looked at me and rolled her eyes and then introduced himself as Tony and would I meet him the next evening and go with him to a wedding reception. I agreed and arrangements made, my daughter and I walked out and went home. I did tell her I wasn't going to turn up and with that said goodnight and I went home to sleep. The next day, I went to check on Steve and found he was having trouble with his neck. It had been very burnt with the radiotherapy but he kept going across the road to the bookies and staying there to try and win on the horses, and most times he did.

I had made up my mind not to turn up for that date, but unbeknown to me, Kelly decided to go in my place. I went about my day but in the evening, I got a phone call from my daughter telling me that she was in another pub just up the road with Tony and had been to this so-called wedding reception and I quote, her words to me were, 'Mum, get up here and have a drink with me now! Tony is with me and he looks so handsome. Don't miss out.'

Oh well, what the hell? I thought to myself, got ready and went to see this so-called Tony, who would not take NO for an answer. Well, I walked in the pub and there he was. We chatted for a while and when closing time came, Kelly went home and I took him to my home. He was pissed and yes, I know what you are all thinking, 'Desperate' comes to mind but I thought it would be fine and when we arrived back at my flat, we talked for a bit then went to bed. He could not do anything because he was so pissed. Just having someone lie next to me felt okay because it had been a couple of years that I had been on my own so I felt it was fine. We woke up and I told him he had to leave. I was not sure about having a friendship with this man and he had a bedsit just down the road, he told me he had separated from his wife and was living alone until he had sorted his life out. Oh my god, could life not be just a little bit okay for me? I don't think I needed to hear this right now. How much more complicated will life be for me? He asked to see me again in a few days and that he would phone before he came to see me. I agreed but wasn't really bothered. Kelly came to see me later on that day and asked how it went. Well, I had no sordid details to tell her but did tell her I was going to see him again later on in the week. One thing did concern me though, the way he told me he drank a lot and that he had been drinking since the age of 13 after his grandad introduced him to vodka. Warning signs clicked in my head but at that time, I ignored them, I wasn't really involved with him, was I?

Things plodded on day by day until one night when I was fast asleep, my phone rang. It was my son and daughter phoning me from the hospital telling me that their dad had phoned for an ambulance as he could not breathe properly and to come quick. I got dressed and got a taxi and went straight to the hospital. Mike and Kelly were there waiting for me and Steve was in the operating theatre. Mike told me his dad could hardly breathe and an ambulance had been called and that's all any of us knew. We saw him being wheeled back to a ward and there was no noisy gasping for breath and he looked peaceful but maybe that was partly due to the anaesthesia. His consultant took us into a side room and told us that the cancer in Steve's throat was inoperable and there was nothing they could do for him. He had also had a tube put into his tummy which was there to administer liquid food as he would never be able to eat again via his mouth. He also told us that he had a tracheotomy which was a tube permanently stitched into his throat, which would help him breathe easier but that the cancer was terminal and although he would be able to go home in a couple of days, the doctor said he would arrange for nurses to visit him in the morning and in the evening to give him his food through his feeding tube and clear his tracheotomy tube twice a day of any mucus or gunge that had built up as it was important that it didn't get clogged up. We all just sat there stunned and crying. We all went home that night, completely exhausted. Kelly was heavily pregnant and I felt so troubled for her as good old Joe, the bastard, had done a runner and didn't want to know after he found out about the baby. Her dad came home a couple of days later. A nurse came with a little suction machine which he had to keep close to him in case it was needed.

She showed Kelly and me how to connect the suction pipe to the tube in his throat if he started struggling to breathe. Kelly was better at it than me so she did it most of the time. Steve never went out of the flat again and he never spoke another word. While all this was going on, I moved Tony into my flat upstairs (first mistake) and we started living together but I never put him on my tenancy agreement. Not that stupid, but stupid enough to have him there in the first place. I took him down and introduced him to Steve and all Steve did was shake hands with him and wrote on a piece of paper, "Look after Hazel." Tony promised he would but looked uncomfortable just being there, and I don't think he wanted me there either as he said that now I was divorced, it wasn't my job.

'Well, you can go fuck yourself mate because for as long as it took, I would be coming and going.' He just stared at me and shut his mouth. He knew I meant business.

Most of the time, Tony was out drinking all day and then came home and went to sleep then did it all over again the next day and the next. I told him he had to find a job or he was gone and at least he did that, getting a job as a delivery driver, working five days a week, which kept him off the beer.

Well, life carried on. Steve didn't improve, he got slowly sicker and kept losing weight. I spent a lot of time at his flat to keep him company and one night, he wrote on his notepad that he would like me to stay the night. I didn't refuse but was a little apprehensive because of his tracheotomy and worried that if anything went wrong, would I be able to handle it without panicking? I didn't think twice actually and said I would stay. I don't care what Tony thought. He was out and he would probably think I was with my daughter as she was very close to having her baby, and he would probably be drunk and not even miss me and I wasn't married to anyone so I was not being unfaithful. I helped Steve to bed that night and then got in and lay next to him. Although he never spoke, his actions spoke volumes to me. Yes, we made love, slowly and went to sleep in each other's arms and he slept peacefully without any problems with his breathing. It felt to me that he knew this would be the last time he ever held me and had me close to him and I think he knew that I knew that too. I sorted him out the next morning and sat him in his chair in front of the telly to wait for the nurses to come and help him with everything. I kissed the top of his head and left to go up one floor to my flat. Tony had just woken up, ready for work and I lied and told him I had been at my daughter's flat as she needed me. He just shrugged and said he was going to work. He had also not moved in completely and had still kept his bedsit because he had quite a few of his belongings still there.

About two weeks passed before I got a phone call from Kelly, saying that she thought she was in labour and could I go to her flat. When I arrived, I could see that she was and got her to hospital as soon as possible. She was put in the Labour ward and I was told that if I wanted to stay with her until after the birth, I could, so the nurses put her in a single room and I had a mattress on the floor next to her bed. She also had a little bathroom to herself and was told by the midwife that if she took a nice warm bath, it would help with the contractions. Well, I ran her a bath, and the contractions kept coming, I rubbed her back and she told me to piss off, not to touch her and was quite grumpy with me as the contractions came closer together. We walked up and down the corridor and she had to stop every so often to do her breathing as her contractions got stronger and once we were back in her room, a nurse came to examine her and said she was just about 9 cm dilated and was taken to the room where she was due to give birth. I never left her side as she was scared because she did not know what to expect and became frightened of the pain. I held one leg and the nurse held the other and all I kept telling her was to push when her contractions came, it didn't take long after that and first I could see the head and the body shortly followed. The nurse cleaned her first baby up, which was a little boy and she lay back totally exhausted. I was allowed to cut the cord which was amazing and it bonded me to him in a strange sort of way. The baby was handed to Kelly but she started being sick so I held him and just gazed at him. Kelly was totally exhausted and spent but asked for her baby boy and holding him tightly, was wheeled back to her room. She came home after a couple of days but was very weak and tired. She tried her best to breastfeed him, but it was obvious that her nipples were so cracked and sore that she cried in pain, so I helped out the best way I could. Eventually, he went onto the bottle and when Kelly felt strong enough, she took little Alfie, yes, his name was Alfie, to see his grandad. I knew deep in my heart that this would be the only time he would hold and see his grandson. She walked into the flat and her dad was hooked up to this suction machine and Kelly told him to hold his arms out and she gently laid his grandson into his arms. 'This is Alfie, Dad,' she said in a quiet voice and although he was weak, he held his first grandson in his arms which I knew would be the last time. He just gazed down at him with love in his eyes and then handed him back to Kelly. It was heartbreaking to watch because I knew that it would not be long before he went to heaven, but at least he had seen him and that's all that mattered.

It was only a few weeks after that when Steve was taken back into hospital for the last time. He was struggling to breathe so the doctors put him in a side room where he was fixed up to an automatic machine that continually sucked cancer and gunge from his throat. My son's second wife visited him and me. Tony, by this time, had come to live with me permanently and told me he didn't want me to keep going to the hospital to see him and I more or less told him to go fuck himself.

I was not happy in the flat where I was living so asked the warden if I could apply for another warden aided flat that I had seen just up the road from where I was living now. Shortly after applying to the council and going to see the property, I asked the warden there if she could put in a good word for me with the council and not long after, I was offered the keys to a second-floor flat there and could go and see it. It was in a better location, I felt safer there and after looking at it, said yes straight away. I moved in 2006 and Tony came too. It was wintertime and cold and I pushed everything I owned up in a shopping trolley, trip after trip after trip. I had already had carpets put down so it was just a case of moving in. I still wasn't sure about Tony but pushed it to the back of my mind and concentrated on settling in and I had my tenancy agreement with just my name on it and it always stayed that way. It was nice and I was happy except I was not happy about Tony not being able to go one day without a drink. He didn't drink indoors but stayed out drinking all day, coming back home pissed at night and either puking up or just going to sleep. Only later, as I got to know him, did he tell me some surprising things about himself. For one start, he was scared to have sex because he got bad headaches afterwards that scared him. I really wanted to bloody laugh but could tell he was serious. Well, that didn't bother me, company was all I needed really. Then another bombshell, wait for it!!! He liked dressing up in women's clothes and always had. He used to go to secondhand shops and buy women's clothes and underwear and actually found some high heeled shoes and got himself a wig. Oh shit! I had heard it all now. He was a middle-aged man for God's sake. I took it all in my stride, wanting to laugh until I cried, not because I have anything against people who wanted to do that, but the fact that I had got hooked up with a man who could not in any way look like a woman and would eventually become a laughing stock. Anyway, more about that later.

Kelly was still living in her little flat just down the road with little Alfie who was about 2–3 months old and I was helping her the best way I could. Tony told me not to visit Kelly's dad in hospital as it wasn't my place, so I did the exact opposite and went to see him when I could. I remember one time when I went to see him and although he was semiconscious, he opened his eyes and recognised me. I hugged him and he pulled me so tight to him and wouldn't let go. I was so close, I could smell the cancer coming from his neck and had a hard job pulling away. I looked into his eyes and could tell he was pretty close to dying. His eyes had a greyish film over them and the skin on his hands as he held mine were almost transparent like you could see through it into his body. I stayed for a while as most of the time he slept and the only noise you could hear was the whooshing of the suction machine. It really was heart-breaking. Only a few nights after that, well it was around 3 am one morning, I got a frantic phone call from a friend of Kelly's telling me that her dad had just died and could I come down to look after Alfie while she went to the hospital. I never moved so quick in my life to get dressed and out of the door, turning to Tony and telling him where I was going. He just muttered something and went back into his drunken sleep and I raced to my daughter's side. She was in bits. I told her to phone a taxi and go and I would look after Alfie. With that said, she was gone. She came back in bits. She was very close to her dad so she was hurting. To cut a long story short, before the funeral, I went to the chapel of rest in the hospital and saw him to say my last goodbye. Mike told me to go and make my peace and to not touch him. 'By the way my son' I kissed him on the lips and told him I loved him. So stuff you, son. I was with him till he passed and I was entitled to say goodbye to him the way I wanted. He looked so at peace, I felt that he wanted to just open his eyes and hold me and say goodbye. That was the last I saw of him, he was now on his next journey, God bless him.

Days passed, we were all grieving and then, shock fucking horror. I was informed by my son that I was not allowed at the funeral or the burial. All the family came up from Kent outside London, but I was excluded from my children's father's funeral. I was upset and grieving and could quietly have punched him in the face. I knew I had to look after Alfie as he was very young but the shock of being told that I could not attend the funeral just broke me yet again. After a while, Kelly phoned me and asked me to bring Alfie down to the church where there was a wake, so I did. I didn't dress in black, I just put Alfie in his pushchair and went into the church where I saw all Kelly's dad's relations who had come up from Kent. I was completely ignored by everyone including the vicar. It felt like I was a Leper in that crowd and I didn't stay long. My son tried to be nice but felt embarrassed that I was there but there was one secret I kept to myself and that was that although he hated me for being there and thought in his head that I had tried to kill him while he was in my womb, he had no idea that his dad's first wife who was pregnant before she went to Australia with her second husband Brian with her third child and did not want it so decided to shove a knitting needle up inside herself to abort the baby she was carrying. It didn't work and V, her third baby was born brain-damaged and disabled and still is to this day. I think he got the mothers mixed up. Mike, if you are reading this, I had an operation to get pregnant with you by Lord Pinker at St Mary's hospital and it was successful. The other mother, your dad's first wife, long before you came along, married to your dad, did the exact opposite and tried to abort your half-sister with a knitting needle for fuck's sake. Your dad told me the reason she was born disabled and it's about time you got your mothers sorted out and stop telling people or your mates in the pub that I tried to kill you. I wanted you, the other wife didn't. Ask God to forgive you for that because your mind is fucked from what you think happened and what did happen and that came from your dad before he died, in fact, a long time before so get your head right and know that I will never forgive you for not letting me go to your dad's funeral but I put fresh flowers on his grave every two weeks. Ask yourself, how many times have you been to visit your dad's grave. NEVER! I hate you for everything you think I have done, but I have done nothing wrong and you need to think about that and go to anger management because you hit your wife, you get too drunk and you have had more than one affair in your marriage. K has been a good wife to you and she has suffered and still does. Well, after that little heart rendering of know all and tell all, Kelly moved again. She rented a two bedroomed house in the street next to me and I was happy for her. We were in touch daily but little did I know that she went on her computer and found a dating site called XXXXXX but ended with fish and got involved with a bloke from Maidstone in Kent. He had his own house and they decided to meet. The thing was, he met her when Tony and I were having a beer in a local pub in Nottingham and Tony was dressed as a woman (God help me for putting up with this stupid shit), and in Kelly walked with this man who she introduced as Adam and he came up to me and shook hands and said, 'I'm going to marry your daughter, I am,' in a proper cocky cockney accent.

Oh really, you knobhead, I don't think so, I thought to myself. What a flashy cockney bastard he seemed to me. I very much had my doubts about him and instantly did not like him one bit. By this time, I had already married Tony in a registrar office in 2009 but was not really happy with the situation but went with the flow. This man who my daughter was involved in suddenly decided to take Kelly and little Alfie to live with him in Maidstone in Kent and I was absolutely heartbroken when she suddenly packed up everything from the house she was living in and got in his van with my grandson and waved me off from the pavement and said goodbye and that she would be happy in a house with this man who she hardly knew. As I waved her off from the front of my flat, I cried until my eyes cried dry tears. She was going so far away and didn't know anyone and it would be so strange for her. She was going with a young six-month-old son. I could see that she was crying like me but she craved company and someone to love but he didn't love her, I knew. I had that bond with her and I knew that she knew, but was on the move, just like me, searching for something that she would never find. It was only later that I found that she was driving away from me into hell. Things happened quickly for her after that. She stayed down there for a few months, I went to visit her and slept downstairs because Alfie was in one of only two bedrooms, and then I came home after being with them for a weekend. She acted like she was the perfect partner for him and I was happy for her but did notice that she was drinking secretly behind her partner's back. I knew at that moment that she was becoming unhappy but kept my mouth shut. Came back to Nottingham on the train and I was knackered. It was around two hundred miles there and the same back. Well, I kept in touch by phone and then all of a sudden, out of the blue, she told me she was going to get married to him and had persuaded him to come back to Nottingham to get married in a church right across the road from me and that she had found a little house in Nottingham to move into and that she was 15 weeks pregnant with knobhead's baby. She missed being near me and wanted to come home to have this baby. (Just like me all over again) History repeats itself, don't you think? His mother found her a wedding dress and arranged for all the family to come and stay in hotels in Nottingham just before the wedding. I had no part in being the mother of the bride and being there for her so the best I could do was book a place for the wedding reception and a honeymoon suite at a posh hotel, otherwise, I had no say in the matter. I did not see her until the day of the wedding, just inside the church and she looked beautiful but I was so unsure this was right. I knew that the prick had his own business and could find work so that was okay but something just didn't sit right with me. It was a cold autumn wedding and, in the church, there were just his family and me and Tony and I looked after Alfie in his pushchair. That was about the size of it. Knobhead's parents looked down their nose at me because I turned up at the church wearing a mini skirt and little top and his side of the family wore PROPER clothes so I don't think that I was in the picture of the day but so what. I was the mother of the bride and my daughter loved me, no matter what. The reception went well and I went home after a while because I was pissed off at the show of it all, so false. After that, same old, same old. The newlyweds went off to live in their new rented house and their life went back to normal as such. He went to work but Kelly wanted a bigger house to rent and she found a big posh one in Nottingham, way beyond their means. Her husband (knobhead) tried to find work but he was out of his league up here in Nottingham and it didn't work for him. The house was huge with a huge monthly rent as well and all of a sudden, he couldn't work. Just a few jobs here and there. My daughter was ready for giving birth and I offered to stay and help out looking after Alfie until after Kelly had her baby. When she went into labour, I moved in for a few days and one day I got a call from the hospital, well, Knobhead actually telling me that she had given birth to a little girl, quite healthy and that Kelly would be home in a couple of days. After this, things went a bit haywire. While I was looking after Alfie and sleeping in the same bedroom as him, the prick she was married to had told Kelly while she was in the hospital that he had had sex with me in the house while she was away giving birth. Shock horror. She told me this later on but what a thing to say about a woman. I really hated him more than anything in the world because I didn't like him and hated that he was my daughter's husband.

Well, of course, this put doubts in her head and she asked me about it later and I told her that I would not touch him with a ten-foot barge pole. I could not stand the man and what annoyed me the most was that he was always walking around the house with his hands down his trousers, fiddling. That made me feel very uncomfortable and much later on, I asked him about that and he said he did not realise he was doing it. He disgusted me to the point that I could have very easily have blown his brains out and he would not have been missed. After that episode, my daughter became unsure of me, but I convinced her that he was a dirty bastard and that he wanted to wind her up on purpose to make her hate me, all the time, walking around the house like the cocky, controlling and up-his-own-arse bastard that I knew him to be. Kelly thought the moon shone out of his arse and before anyone knew it, "even me", they had done a moonlight flit back to his house in Maidstone and set up his family there once again, back on his own turf so to speak. It broke my heart but worse was to come. Kelly started drinking heavily because she was being controlled, just like me. I can't believe how history repeated itself.

Chapter Twelve
To Hell and Back

Kelly was settled, (I knew different) and Tony and myself used to go down to Maidstone every so often just for a couple of days. Tony took him out drinking at night, which Kelly hated so she and I started drinking together at her home. By the time the men got home, we were pissed and so were they. And they would always have arguments before bed and in bed. I heard everything and I felt so sorry for Kelly because her husband was such a control freak and dominating that she always bowed to whatever he said. Now, where have I heard that before? Reminds me of me, many years ago in London! Her husband didn't treat Alfie very well either, probably because he didn't belong to him but adored his little baby girl. When we went into the town centre, if Alfie was being naughty, Adam used to pull his pants down in the middle of a busy street just to punish him. My heart was breaking but I could not say a word. He also used to bully him indoors as well and shout at him constantly. It was like Alfie was invisible. I hated that man so much and the day he drove us to the train station, Tony said goodbye and turning to me told me that he never wants to come and see them again and that he felt like taking Kelly's husband's head off because he treated Kelly and Alfie so bad. I did not go down so often but found out later that Kelly began borrowing money from people she had got to know as her twat of a husband would not give her any shopping money or anything, and then she had people after her because she could not pay it back. He left her without any money, so she just borrowed from others or ran up bills in the shop and mainly it was for bottles of wine. She seemed to me that she wanted to stay drunk all the time just to blot out the bastard she had married.

One day, I was walking to my local shop and got a phone call from her. She told me that there would be a train ticket waiting for me at Nottingham train station and could I come straight away. She was crying and so I turned around, went and packed a bag and told Tony where I was going and would see him when I got back. He didn't care because he was always out drinking so he didn't look too bothered. I was so tired and had a two-hundred-mile train journey in front of me but I would go to the ends of the earth for my daughter and she knew I would go to her. Well, I arrived at Maidstone station and outside there was a man who told me that he had come to pick me up and take me to Kelly's house. I did not know this man and was a bit wary but he assured me and said Kelly needed my help. That was enough for me and off we went. I found Kelly, huddled in a corner of the sofa, crying and she told me that Mr Macho Man had left her and gone to live with his mum. Two men had kicked in the door and slapped her around and demanded the money she owed them, amongst other people, but she had talked them down and they left and so there she was, in a house that was not hers, left with two young children and nothing else and she was drunk. I sat with her, held her and told her that I would stay a few days. Got the kids to bed, made sure the door was locked as much as I could and then told Kelly to go to bed.

The next morning, I started cleaning the house. I went up to her bedroom and straightened things up, deciding to look under the bed. I was so shocked to find about fifty miniature empty wine bottles hidden under there. I got a black bin bag and put them all in there, and then went around the house, searching. I found bottles hidden everywhere, kitchen, living room, just about everywhere. Now I knew that she was unhappy and relied on drinks to take the mental agony of what she was suffering at the hands of the husband (bastard) to just take the pain away, but all the time, keeping house and looking after two little children. I really think that is when she became an alcoholic. She had no excuses for what I had found but told me that she needed her drink and also wanted her husband back, regardless of what he had put her through. My heart was breaking and I had no solution except to tell her she needed to come home. She was alone with no one and I was 200 miles away. Anyway, I could not stay down there forever and told her I had to go home and did ask her to re-think what I had suggested to her. She told me she was staying to see if he came back but would come up for a visit soon. I told her sooner rather than later and that she might be in danger if she stayed.

It was with a heavy heart that I left to go back home that day but Kelly told me she would be okay and that she would get sorted, but she wanted to stay and wait to see if the wanker came back. I felt so sorry for her and hoped that it would not be long before I saw her in Nottingham soon. It was sooner than I thought. It was a cold January 23, 2013 and she phoned to tell me that she was here at a friend's flat in the next block and would be around soon. It was such a surprise and I was excited. Tony was out as usual but I did phone him and tell him to come back early as Kelly was here and I was going to cook a roast dinner to celebrate. She bought the kids 'round to see me and I cuddled them so tightly. God! How I had missed them. She had also bought around a couple of bottles of wine to have with dinner. Oh! Thinking to myself, I had better keep my eye on her with that. Well, Tony, the pisshead came home early and we all had a roast chicken dinner and the kids played and Kelly seemed calmer for a change. We both drank wine and she decided to take the kids back to her friend's house and put them to bed saying she would come back later when they were asleep and the three of us could play a board game.

Well, it got to around teatime, just before 5 pm to be exact and I decided to go to my local shop for a packet of cigarettes just in case we ran out. It was cold and dark and that night my life changed forever. Next to my block of flats was a one-way street, very narrow, with no street lighting at all. The roads were very quiet and after I picked up my ciggies, just had to walk a few hundred yards back home. The streets were empty and quiet because it was winter and cold. I was wearing a bright red coat, warm and cosy and the tiny one-way street was empty and the main street going across the bottom was so silent. I was looking forward to spending time with my daughter but that was not about to happen. No cars, no nothing and just as I had crossed this little tiny one-way street and was about to step up onto the pavement, all I could see were two big headlights in front of me. Never heard a car or anything and the next thing I knew or rather felt was an impact and there I was, flying through the air and instinctively putting my hand up to the left side of my head to protect my brain because I knew I was going to hit the road hard.

Don't even know why I did that but it must have just been instinct. I landed on my left side, in the grit on the road and it was only then that I realised that a car had hit me full impact. I just lay there, and I could taste blood in my nose and running down my face. I called for help and could not move. The next thing I knew, there was a man and woman bending down to help me by wiping the blood from my face. It was seconds before I heard the ambulance and although I didn't realise it at the time, a police car had turned up at the scene as I just lay there bleeding onto the road. My daughter had been told about what had happened and came racing to see what had happened to me. The police had the driver in the back of the police car and as far as I know, she was trying to get into the police car to kill the man that had hit me. She was going absolutely apeshit but the police kept her away. As this was all going on, I was told I had an open fracture to my left ankle, which I found out later, my ankle was up the road so there was a lot of blood, but when the paramedics touched my right leg, which had not had a scratch on it or blood coming from it, I was screaming in pain and my daughter knew that there was something wrong with that leg, although it looked normal. I remember being put in the ambulance, my fucking drunken husband coming with me and Kelly getting a taxi and following behind. I was blue lighted to hospital but not before, when I was screaming in pain on the road about my right leg, which I was told had not got any blood or marks on it that the pain was unbearable. My left ankle bone was half-way up the road and that was an open fracture and I could not feel a thing with that, but it was my right leg that was puzzling the paramedics. It was perfectly straight and looked normal.

As soon as I arrived at the hospital, I was rushed into the Resus room where a lot of doctors were waiting for me. I could not move, my face was covered in blood, seeping up into my hair and they had to cut off all my clothes, my brand new bright red coat, my jeans and jumper, everything right down to my panties. I was screaming with pain in my right leg and by that time my daughter had arrived and screaming at the doctors told them there was something wrong with that leg otherwise I would not be screaming like that so I was rushed for an MRI scan.

Well, the MRI scan showed that I didn't have any damage to my brain but I had a broken nose, fractured pelvis, fractured scapula, open fractured left ankle and lo and behold, the long bone going down my right leg, from the knee down had been broken completely in two and that's why it did not show up any damage on the outside and why it left the doctors puzzled as to why I was screaming in pain. The doctors and orthopaedic consultant came to see me and both my legs encased in those blow-up leg protectors, I was taken to the high dependency unit and put in a bed for five hours until the early hours of the next morning, when I was due for some sort of surgery. I kept going in and out of consciousness during this time and Kelly went to sleep in a waiting room somewhere. That drunken bastard I was married to went home, the knob had slept in his bed but it was at this moment in my life, I knew who loved me the most. It was 5 am in the morning when I was taken down to surgery and Kelly was right there, crying and I looked her straight in the eyes and told her to go back down south with the kids and go home because I would not be going anywhere for the time being. She sobbed her heart out and did not want to leave me but I told her it would all work out okay and that I was in safe hands. God knows why I said that as I was 65 years old and might die. As we arrived at the theatre doors, Kelly had to say goodbye to me and she was wrecked but she had to let me go. I kissed her and told her I loved her and to go back home. As I was pushed through the door by the nurses, I turned my head and saw her crying and shouting that she loved me. That broke my heart because I did not know whether I would survive this. Well, I did survive the operation and when I finally woke up, I was back in my bed with my left leg strung up on a pulley that was over my bed. I gazed down at my left leg all bleary-eyed and found two huge rods pushed through from one side of my leg and out the other. Just my ankle was bandaged and my right leg had a dressing all the way down the front and later I found out that I had a huge scar down the centre which I saw later had clips in it, all the way down. I was told not to move much as the doctors wanted my pelvis to mend. A few hours later, the consultant came to see me and give me the devastating news that they had not yet fixed my ankle and had put the rods through my leg to hold it onto my ankle as they didn't know how to fix it. I had no ankle bone and they told me that they had to go away and come up with a plan to either fix my ankle back onto my leg or amputate. *Oh my God,* thinking to myself, *I can't survive without a foot. I can't live without my fucking foot, I'm not that old and I have things to do with my life.* The consultant just looked at me and walked off. This was going to be one hell of a long stay on this ward but somehow I found the strength to keep going. I lay in that bed for eight weeks, going through four more surgeries, each time, coming out with my left leg still connected. Each time I came through surgery, first the rods came out, then screws were put into my ankle, then rods put up into both legs, then more screws were added and finally, my left leg was encased in plaster with tubes coming from it which every so often did things to the inside of the plaster. The nurses were superb, and one of them even washed the blood from my hair while still in the bed. I was told not to move much because the doctors wanted my pelvis to heal. The physiotherapist came every day and I had to do small exercises in the bed every day.

After eight weeks, I was told by the nurses that I could not go home until I could learn how to boardslide. That meant, sliding my bum across a board to a wheelchair, that had been specially made for me with bits that came off to allow me to do this. I was not allowed to put either leg onto the floor so that was the reason. The physio ladies came every day and watched while I did this and also told me that when I arrived home, there would be a commode on wheels waiting for me and also a chair in the shower room and I had to boardslide from one to the other, all the time. Fuck me, that was a tall order as I wasn't very strong in body as my muscles had wasted from being in a bed for so long. Luckily, there was a sofa bed in the living room so all that was sorted. I was told I had to go everywhere in my wheelchair and not to get my left leg wet if I took a shower. That was fine and before I left I asked if I could wheel myself down in the lift and go outside for some fresh air. I had a friend visit at the time and was told she could push me.

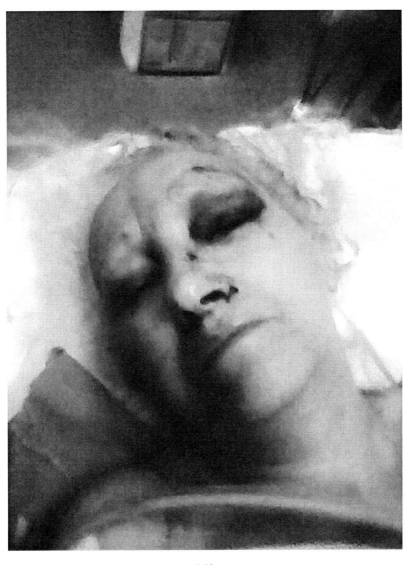

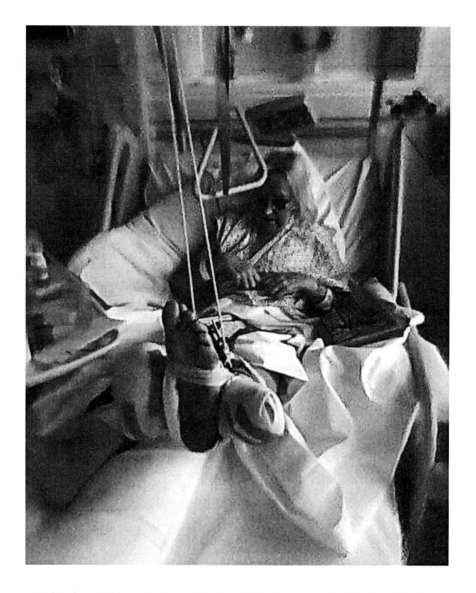

Well, after eight weeks in one bed, using bedpans and not being able to move, it was like heaven and secretly, I wanted a smoke. The fresh air was just beautiful and the smoke even better, but it gave me a head rush and I asked my friend to take me back to the ward. I felt very weak and not used to being out of my bed at all. Well, the day arrived when I was told I could go home in an ambulance but had to go back in March for more surgery.

I had to go back for surgery in March and was told the consultant had decided that I needed a bone graft and he was going to take some bone from my hip and insert it into my ankle to make it a bit stronger. That meant another three months in my wheelchair, board sliding and literally living from my wheelchair. *Okay! I could handle that,* I thought to myself. I've come this far and never thought I would make it. Anyway, the ambulance turned up to take me home and I said such a big thank you to all the staff that had got me through my pain and my injuries and told them I would see them in March. Well, when the ambulance got me home and wheeled me through my door and into the living room in my wheelchair, I found the drunken wanker stuck up a ladder wallpapering the living room, not looking too bothered about me being thereafter the last eight weeks in hospital. I had learned how to push myself around in my wheelchair by now and after saying thank you to the ambulance man, I wheeled myself over to the living room window and parked myself there.

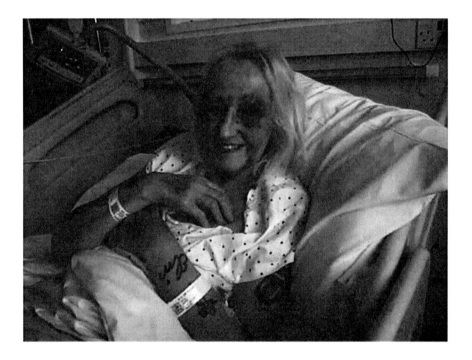

Tony didn't look too happy that I was home and shortly I told him that I needed to use the toilet and could he push me into the shower room. To be quite honest, I don't think he gave a fuck but did what I asked, all be it unwillingly. He just left me there to cope on my own. I dismantled the sides of the wheelchair and slid myself over to the toilet then slid myself back, then, I had to shout for him to wheel me back into the living room. He was not a happy chappie. I board-slided onto my sofa bed and asked him to make me something to eat. I was exhausted. Well, from that day, he had to do everything for me. He had to cook, clean, take me to the shower and even had to empty my commode which I knew fucked him off completely. He didn't expect that, and I felt useless. Also, he had my bank card and used it when he wanted to and although it had only my name on it, I had to give him my pin number and let him get on with it. Well, reluctantly, he sort of looked after me but I could tell that he didn't like doing the personal things for me and without his help, I was fucked.

Every day, he left me for a few hours to go drinking and then had to come and look after me and that pissed him right off but time passed and it was soon March and I went back into the hospital again for my bone graft. Another bloody surgery and I was so very scared of being put to sleep in case I never woke up. This time I was in the hospital for a week and when I came 'round, I had a normal plaster cast on my left leg and the dressing was taken from my right leg and I looked down and all I was looking at was a long line of staples holding my scar together. I was now told during that week that I could try and use a walking frame and go to the toilet on the ward. The first time I did this, there was a nurse with me and I was told I had to sort of hop and not put my left leg on the ground. How the fuck was I going to manage this. Well, I did get to the loo but felt very faint and thought I would pass out at one point but I was strong in my mind and did do it and it felt so good.

After a week, I was allowed to go home. I could use my walking frame around the flat but mostly I had to use my wheelchair at all times. I had learned how to use my chair but it was hard and mostly I had to rely on "HIM". He was really out of his comfort zone with me and didn't like doing stuff for me at all, and I learnt how to go and do stuff in the kitchen by myself because he was out drinking most of the time, and I also learnt how to use the commode and sit on it and shuffle myself into the bathroom and empty it myself. As time went on, things stayed the same until one night, there was a knock at the door. Tony answered it because I was yet again on my sofa bed. I heard him say come in and there was my daughter with a bunch of flowers and told me she had put everything she owned in bin liners and come back permanently with the kids to live. She had left the prick of a husband down south and was never going back. She told me that when she went back down south from the hospital, twat face had changed the lock on the door so she couldn't get in so she phoned her taxi driver friend from Nottingham to come and when he arrived, he kicked the door in and she raced around the house collecting everything she could and piled everything she could in the back of his taxi and drove off with the kids and came home where she belonged. At the time, I didn't know this, the shit face was having to get my food ready, and I eventually went back for a check-up in hospital and told that I had to have my plaster changed every two weeks but I was okay with that. I could use my commode in the kitchen and shuffle and hop to the bathroom by myself and start to recover, although I had to still board slide from bed to wheelchair to commode, but I was getting there and started to feel stronger each day. My plaster was changed every two weeks.

Finally, I was told that the plaster on my left leg could come off for good but I would have to wear one of those huge hospital boots but could take it off to have a shower and was told to use my wheelchair most of the time. I also had a walking frame delivered to my flat and was told to exercise as much as possible. I watched the nurse saw my plaster away and looked down in horror at my leg. It was so thin and shrunken and the skin was peeling away from my leg and there were scars all over my lower leg and ankle. I was so shocked, I was speechless but the nurse reassured me that with time and gentle exercise, it would soon begin to fill out. I was taken back home in an ambulance and I could finally organise myself. I had to learn how to walk again and it took me a year of struggle and also had to come to terms with the fact that I would never walk properly again. I had one leg shorter than the other so had a permanent limp but it was a small price to pay to have my life. Tony, the drunken bastard didn't want to help me anymore now that I could shuffle around more. He was out drinking every day again and slowly I got my routine back.

The first thing I asked my husband for was my bank card. It had only my name on it and I wanted to take charge of my life again. He just stood in front of me while I sat on my commode seat in the kitchen and glared. It was my old age pension card and I wanted it back. He just stood in front of me and took it from his wallet and slammed it down on the floor in front of me. I did not give a shit at that time, I wanted what belonged to me. I bet he had a field day with that card while I was in that hospital bed for eight weeks so now the hard-drinking man had no source of income, except the little bit of pocket money I gave him each week. What a selfish prick he was.

One day my daughter came in with a huge smile on her face, computer stuck under her arm. I was lying on my sofa bed resting my legs and she sat on the end of the sofa and told me she had a wonderful surprise for me. 'Mum! I've found your sister and your two brothers on Facebook.'

I lay there with my mouth open. 'You're fucking kidding me.' She opened up her computer and turned it around to face me and there staring at me was a photo of my sister looking at me. That's not her, it can't be, eyes popping out of my head. She looked older but beautiful. Then she clicked on the next photo of my brother Danny, then she clicked again and there was my brother Jimmy looking at me. Older, but both my brothers looked so handsome. I was speechless, tears rolling down my face. After 43 years, there they were and I could not believe Kelly had done that for me. After that, I left it to Kelly to get in touch with them and she sent photos of me and it was a while before I received emails from them. They could not believe it either and at first, I didn't know how to answer them. After all these years, there they were and I thought they were all dead because I knew that my birth mother had taken my sister over to America and also had my two brothers over there. We all had different fathers and on my birth certificate, there was no mention of my real dad. Mother certainly did get around. I kept in touch with them many times and they were shocked to hear of my accident.

Meanwhile, I had the all-clear from my consultant and that if I used my big boot and my walking frame, I just had to go have a check-up and x-ray of my legs every six weeks. During this time, while Kelly and the children were still living with her friend at the next block to mine, something horrendous happened to me. It was a life-or-death situation with me "AGAIN" but this time, I was fighting for my life in a different way.

Chapter Thirteen
Attempted Murder

Well, sitting there in my kitchen one evening, alone, as fuck face had been out drinking all day, on my commode which was a seat as well, and had my walking frame in front of me. I felt quite comfy and was watching television from the doorway when in staggered the drunk. He fell onto the sofa in a drunken stupor so I just left him and carried on watching the telly. Eventually, he surfaced and we started talking sort of. He came into the kitchen and got a glass from the kitchen and then went into the cupboard behind the sofa and produced a one-litre bottle of vodka and sat down again in his corner. You have to remember that he was still drunk but poured himself a shot of straight vodka from the bottle. *Oh, bloody hell,* I thought to myself and stayed put in the kitchen and didn't speak to him. As the night wore on, I tried to have a conversation with the drunken bum but he said nothing and just kept drinking. All of a sudden, he got up from the sofa, came over to me, got hold of my walking frame and threw it across the room, knowing that I could not and was told not to walk without it. He threw it so far across the room that I could not move without it and could not reach it. I froze as he pushed by me and I heard him go to the knife rack and the next thing I felt was him behind me while I was sitting on my commode chair, wielding a 12-inch carving knife over my head trying to stab me, yes, literally trying to stab me in the head and neck. I put my hands up instinctively, trying to stop him and began screaming for my life. He didn't utter a word, just kept trying to push the knife down into my head and neck. I pushed his arms upwards and used all my strength to push the knife away from my body, screaming and screaming, but no one came to help me. I was pleading and begging and praying for my life then suddenly, he walked into the living room, stripped naked, lay on his stomach with the point of the knife under him pointing up towards his stomach. I didn't say a word but my silent tears fell down my cheeks and my heart felt like it would burst from my chest because it was beating so hard. Oh my God, what could I do? I was helpless and terrified and could not move. I sat, stiff and rigid with fear, not speaking and not moving and very very frightened. I really thought I was going to die that night. Suddenly, dragging himself back to his corner of the sofa, still holding the knife, staring at me, he threw the knife onto the carpet, picked up the bottle of vodka and his glass, turned and asked if I was coming to bed. Quietly, I answered that I was just going to finish watching my film then I would come to bed. He staggered off and I knew that he would soon pass out so I just sat in the kitchen for the longest time, not moving, hardly breathing and waiting until I knew he had passed out because I could hear him snoring. I slowly shuffled across the living room from the kitchen and went to retrieve my walking frame and then slowly shuffled back towards the kitchen. I was so terrified and in shock that I sat in that chair in the kitchen all night and never closed my eyes, in case he woke up and came at me again. I was shaking, I was cold but I sat in that chair all night until it began to get light and I waited for the community room to be unlocked.

Very quietly, I got to my feet, legs feeling like jelly and as quietly as I could, I walked slowly and quietly to the door, which was next to the bedroom door. I got myself slowly to the lift at the end of the corridor and went down two floors and made my way to the room where people gathered for breakfast. I took myself off to a side room and phoned my daughter to come straight away and that it was important. I also did not realise that I had picked up the knife and wrapped it in a plastic bag on the way out. Kelly came quickly and I told her what had happened and she called the police straight away and told them to come and talk to me. The police took the knife away and went to arrest him. I did ask them to get my house keys from him and as I sat in the community room, I saw the police take him and put him in the back of the police car. One policeman came back and handed me my door keys and told me someone would be back later to take a statement from me, and also I asked to get a restraining order against him so that he would not come back and try to hurt me again. I was told it would be sorted that day and later, I did get a visit from the police where I made a statement and was also told that he would not be allowed anywhere near the area or else he would be arrested on the spot.

I gave my statement and was assured that the drunk would not be coming near me and that it would be going to court. I breathed a sigh of relief. After the police had left, I knew what I was going to do. My walking frame was on wheels with a basket on the front, so I slowly went to the cupboard behind one of the sofas and opened the door. I was absolutely gobsmacked at what I was looking at. There must have been fifteen one-litre bottles of vodka on the shelves and I knew this was going to be a long job but slowly, bottle after bottle, I put the bottles, a few at a time, pushed them to the kitchen and emptied them down the sink, then I slowly put them a few at a time, down the corridor to the chute room, where people put their rubbish and threw them away. Because of my injuries, I had to be careful and go very slowly, but after a lot of journeys to the rubbish room, I got rid of the last one. There was no more alcohol in the flat. I felt so much better after that but was tired out. Now I was on my own, I had a lot of time to think.

Anyway, I started to feel guilty about everything. Was I the cause of the attack??? Was it too much for him to look after me? And then I started to feel very guilty. I began writing a letter to the court and when the court date came, I had decided to write to the judge before the case came before him asking him to be lenient with my husband and that I was sure he didn't mean it. The court date came and I went to court in a taxi that took my wheelchair. I asked the usher to pass my letter to the judge and I had also written, begging the judge not to send him to prison but let him come home as I wanted to give him one more chance. I thought to myself, was I being stupid? Had I been groomed? (NO.) Did I want companionship? YES. Did I feel sorry for him? YES! All these things going around in my head. I was sitting in my wheelchair downstairs when all of a sudden, a lady came downstairs and took me into a private little room. She told me she was the judge and talked to me about what had happened to me at home. She mentioned domestic violence and tried to persuade me to change what I had said. I thought about what she had said to me and still told her that I wanted him home. She left and I just stayed downstairs and waited and waited. Finally, he came towards me, and my heart started to beat faster. He explained that he had been given a two-year suspended sentence, one year's probation and a fine. He looked happy, but I think that the judge wanted to send him to prison and that's why she came to see me. Domestic violence at that time had started to be noticed by the government but the stupid twat that I was, decided to give him another chance.

My daughter thought I was crazy but gave him the benefit of the doubt. No one will ever believe this but he wheeled me out of the court and found the nearest pub and ordered a drink. We sat there for ages, him drinking pints and me just one glass of wine and then I told him I wanted to go home. He found a taxi to take a wheelchair and we went home. I thought to myself, well at least he won't be drinking fucking vodka, will he?

We arrived home and when he saw what I had done with all of his precious vodkas, he began to get angry until I reminded him that all I would do was make one phone call and he stayed quiet after that. It was 2014 and I wanted to go see my brothers and sister in America so on a whim, I borrowed £2000 from a loan company, booked a ticket to Washington DC and got myself ready and packed to go and meet up with my birth family for the first time in 43 years, thanks to my daughter finding them for me.

My God, what an adventure I had. I was by then just limping on my poorly legs and when I walked through the doors at the airport, there were my two brothers, holding up a sign saying "HI SIS, WELCOME". I limped up to them and just threw my arms around them. My god, what emotion there was. We were all crying and they were both now in their '60s but were just the same as I remembered them in Spain. We couldn't stop crying and it was so strange because they had American accents. I was to stop at Danny's house with his lady friend Dorothy and I really was so exhausted, but it didn't stop us all having a glass of wine and going out onto the balcony of this beautiful house and talking forever, even if it was past 10 pm at night. I was so tired so was shown to my room and I had my own bathroom too. It was so perfect. Jimmy my younger brother was staying for a few days and I could not wait for the next day. I wanted a good night's sleep but found myself waking up at four in the morning because of the time change from the UK, crept downstairs and in the kitchen I found the teabags and made a cuppa and sat out on the balcony in the dark, just happy and safe and home. My oldest brother Danny came down and saw me and came to sit with me and we just talked. He did ask me if I remembered anything about when I run off from the villa in Spain and I did reply that I had a vague idea.

I said I remembered my birth mother and Dan's father screaming at each other and that she accused him of fancying me because I reminded him of my birth mother when she was young and I was also walking around in a bikini all day, sunbathing all day. Danny went quiet and said that it was true and I ran off and lived on the streets. After getting that out the way, he told me that my mother had died of a heart attack in the nineties. He gave me my mother's wedding ring and I thanked him for it and wore it for a long time until I decided to put it in my daughter's wish box to pass on to her after I was gone. I had the most wonderful eight days and was shown around Washington, the White House and the zoo and everywhere. I was told that Sandra my sister was driving up to stay the next day to see me and when I stood outside the house, I saw her and thought how old she had got. She was still my sister and still posh but was two years older than me and had gotten old, like all of us. I didn't have much time to spend with her because she was going home the next day. It was hard to see her go but I told her I would be back soon and would come to see where she lived. I was treated like a queen while I was there. I was taken out for breakfast and then out for an evening meal. It was so lovely but eight days passed very quickly and I had to come back home to England. The goodbye was very emotional and a lot of tears ran down our faces but I had to walk away and turned to wave to my brother and then didn't stop crying until I got on the plane. The flight was fine but no one was at the airport to meet me so I struggled across London on my own and got the train to Nottingham.

Guess who was at the station to meet me at Nottingham? The shit I had kept out of prison and he was drunk! YES, drunk as a fart and guess what? The first place he took me to was a pub because he reckoned I looked tired. I thought to myself, *Yes, I was tired and my legs hurt and all I wanted to do was go home and go to bed and sleep, but no.* We ended up having a drink. Well, he had quite a few actually, then I put my foot down and told him I was going home. I think then that he realised that he had fucked up and we got a taxi home. I didn't even unpack but went straight to bed. I didn't give a shit to be quite honest as I was worn out and had jet lag. After that, life went on as normal, whatever normal was with Sir.

I asked him one day if he would stop drinking and choose me and he told me he chose the drink. Well, I wasn't shocked so decided to live my own life. I had my compensation money by then and decided to take off. For many years, I had wanted to collect a COCO-DE-MER. A coconut from the sea and the only place to find it was the Seychelle Islands so I booked and went there for eight days. I travelled to the island of Praslin where the forest was and walked through it. They were very precious coconuts and the forest where they grew was the only place on earth and guarded by soldiers with guns in case anyone tried to steal them. There were the females, and they looked like a woman's private parts and separate trees that grew catkins, about two feet long and myth had it that at night when in darkness, the male catkins sent their spawn to the females and they grew into these huge coconuts looking like a female pussy. Well, I bought one and had to have a special license to bring it out of the country of MAHE. I stayed at the most wonderful hotel and had a beer with a famous male actor who was with his manager and bodyguard. All he kept talking about was his home in Scotland. The most embarrassing thing was, I had seen him in many films but didn't know his name until I googled it and found out who it was.

How thick was I not to know this man but when I sent a picture to my kids, they recognised him straight away and give me a bollocking for not getting his autograph. I stayed at a great hotel and could just wake up and walk straight onto the sand. I was crippled, limping but built up the courage to go on the back of a jet ski, holding on tight, with a life jacket on, telling this boy I could not swim, but he just smiled and told me I would be safe. He took me right out to sea, around all the posh yachts and back to shore. My legs were still fucked, but I found the courage to do it. It was wonderful. I came home and today, my COCO-DE-MER is on a special wooden stand, with the licence, standing next to my television. I'm pleased I did that. After that, there was no stopping.

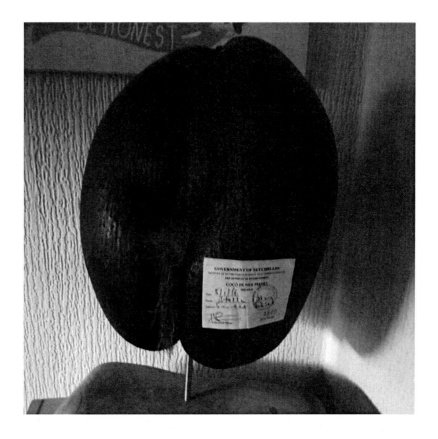

Coco De Mer

154

Even with my crooked legs, I went to Cape Verde and Zanzibar and Africa and up until 2019, kept going back to see the Villa in Spain where I used to live. I don't think I was ever home much before I took off again. The drunk didn't care. If I wasn't there, he could drink himself stupid and I was never in the country to see him pissed. It was 2015, I got a call from my brother Danny in the states telling me that my sister had suffered a stroke and was in the hospital and believe you me, I never packed my case so quick in life. I was on that plane and gone.

I arrived in Washington yet again and was met by my brother, who told me that Sandra had been living out of her car and she had been under enormous pressure but hadn't told anyone. She was in the hospital and after a rest, the next day, I was taken to see her. There she was, lying in a hospital bed. She seemed okay but when she hugged me, she started talking and sometimes, gobbledygook came out of her mouth. Some words I could not understand, some sentences I had to finish for her and I hugged her so close. No matter what she had done in her life, no matter how stuck up and proud she had been with her life, no one deserved this. She was older and thinner and weaker and after I had stayed with her for the longest time, I had to leave her there and go back to Danny's house. He then told me that she had also been diagnosed with Alzheimer's and dementia as well as the stroke. I was in bits and although I only stayed for a few days, going to see her every day, I knew I would not see her again for some reason and I was right. A few months later, I received a call from my brother only to tell me that from the hospital she had been transferred to a small nursing home where one of the staff had found her collapsed in the shower and it was found that she had another stroke. She was back in hospital again and with a lot of medical help, she came through that one but still had dementia. I found out that she would be transferred back to her nursing home as she was not safe to be on her own. She was very well looked after but not allowed to go out on her own so my brother sometimes took her out locally in the car to a bookshop or for coffee. I got regular updates and Danny told me that she repeated herself all the time and asked the same questions she had only asked a few minutes before. I felt heartbroken because I knew I would not be able to see her again and realised she was my blood and I loved her. It was the last time I went to America but she is still with us, and I thank God for giving her the strength to not give up.

Meanwhile, my daughter had moved house yet again and was living just a short bus ride away from me. She was such a gipsy, never staying in one place for long. She was now a single mum and I went to see her nearly every day. Must admit though, she pulled a fast one on me one day. She asked if I could go with my friend and look after the two kids for a few hours. She had to go to a meeting about her drinking, or so I believed. Anyway, little did I know that she had gone to meet a man. I later found out he lived in Chesterfield and little did I know that she had met him on a dating site, because when she finally got back home, dragging him through the door behind her, he shook my hand, told me he was pleased to see me and told me he was Kelly's councillor. I just smiled and told him he was full of bullshit but as I scrutinised him, I thought, well, he's a good-looking guy, he was sort of a Kelly guy, and he was well dressed and very polite to me but I did not believe a bloody word that came out of his mouth. He had obviously been word trained on the way home as to what to say by my devious little daughter As I went to leave, I took her to one side and told her to make sure he didn't hurt her or break her heart because she had been through hell already and I didn't want her to suffer that again. Well, he stayed and stayed and she was happy, so happy in fact that she got pregnant almost straight away. Fuck me, well that said to me that birth control had not been invented for Kelly. That was bloody quick but they seemed happy. Tom seemed to treat her well and looked like he was in for the long haul so I was happy. My daughter so reminded me of me, first meet, first date and at it like rabbits (can't blame her, she was young), and it bought back memories of me with my first love. Once done, never forgotten. Well, she got fatter and fatter and they lived in a decent house but on the day she went into labour, I raced over there and as she was getting in the taxi with Tom. The landlord, the dope-smoking bastard was serving her with an eviction notice. I had two little crying children holding on to me. I looked at Kelly and told her to go have her baby and that the house would still be here when she got back. Tom climbed into the taxi with her and she was crying and also having contractions. I told Kelly I would take care of it and not to worry. I had my friend to back me up and once the taxi had left, turned to the private landlord and told him that my daughter would be coming back to this house with her new baby and pointed my finger so close to his nose that it nearly poked his snot away from his body, told him in no uncertain words that the house stays as it is. A new baby would be coming back to this house and if he had anything else to do, I would personally make it so that he would never walk again. He was a young dope-smoking bastard who did not give a shit as he was stoned most of the time and if he did anything while I was living in that house with her two other children in it, he would personally be pushed out of it in a wheelchair.

He stuttered and stammered and looked at me with glazed eyes, stoned out of his head but agreed that he would not come near the house until after my daughter had had the baby. After? I questioned, it would be quite a while after I told him. When they had found another home, then they would move and until then, I just looked him straight in the stoned grinning face of his and told him to fuck off. He knew I think, by looking at my eyes that I meant business. He left and I continued to look after Alfie and Gwen and later that night, I had a phone call from Kelly's other half telling me I was a grandma again. She had given birth to a healthy little girl and named her Frances. She was beautiful, tiny, with bronze skin and dark hair, just like her daddy.

Well, Tom came home to look after the kids and I went straight to the hospital to see my newborn granddaughter. It felt wonderful to hold her in my arms. Kelly had a normal birth but looked so tired and pale. I left to go home and her boyfriend looked after the kids until she came home two days later. Well, the landlord was still on the case, stoned out of his head and presented them with an eviction order. Well, I shoved him out the door and got on to the council straight away. I explained that my daughter had just had a baby, only a few weeks old, was due to be evicted and had nowhere to go. Well, my sweet-talking did the trick and they told my Kelly that they had a place to rent in Bestwood Village with three bedrooms. Well, Kelly made the move there and then, despite the stone head bastard landlord. They got a van, late at night and legged it leaving behind all the crap they didn't want so it was up to the landlord to get rid of the shit. He deserved it, the bastard.

The house was lovely. They settled in and when Fran was about two years old, my daughter and her boyfriend decided to get married and in 2016 that's what happened. This time, I was the mother of the bride and I paid for everything. I went with Kelly and she had a custom-made bridal gown. I ordered an old-fashioned car to take her to the registrar office in the Council House at the market square in Nottingham. I paid for the wedding reception and the bridal room at a hotel. I also paid for my son and his family to stay in a hotel for the night. I paid for the bridesmaids' dresses and the only glitch was that my son wanted his half-brother to fly from Australia to give Kelly away. I soon put my bloody foot down about that. For one thing, I didn't like him for being a bastard to his first wife, for smashing my cat's head in with a spade and for his real mother for trying to abort her third child by shoving a knitting needle up inside her to try and get rid of her third child which didn't work and the baby turned out to be brain damaged and turned out to be autistic. Mothers getting mixed up again, I think.

Kelly wanted her two uncles to give her away. My brothers from America. Lots of arrangements there to happen then, and I didn't know it until after that my youngest brother Jimmy had had a small stroke but got over it quite quickly and so all arrangements made, it was a go. Kelly and Tom arranged to get married on my birthday and when Kelly knew the date that her two uncles were arriving soon a certain day by train at Nottingham station, she wanted to be there. She had never met them and only seen photos of them but two days before the wedding, she was there on the platform at the station waiting for the train to pull in from London. As we all stood there waiting, she recognised them and started running to them while we all just stood there. 'I can see them, oh my god, there they are.'

The rest of us saw nothing, but she knew. It was so wonderful to see her walking down the platform, hugging my brothers who she had only seen in photos. They were her true blood uncles and she could not stop crying and then we all hugged and cried. Such a big moment for us all, especially Kelly. Guess what though, although they met Tony for the first time, we all walked out of the station and where do you think he took us all, luggage and all? THE FUCKING PUB across the road. Everyone was exhausted but we sat outside and as luck would have it, I took Danny and Jimmy a few yards down from the pub and showed them where 85, Queens Drive was and that was where Mum lived and where I was born.

They took photos and went back to finish our drinks and then Kelly's uncles said they were going to their respective hotels as they were very tired. We all went our separate ways and promised to meet up the next day, one day before the wedding. This time I was at Kelly's house.

The bridesmaids were all dressed. My daughter was dressed in a magnificent dress and veil and was absolutely looking beautiful. I went in the car with my bridesmaids and the kids and waited at the register office for this beautiful antique car to drive up. Out stepped the bride and my two brothers, one on each arm. She looked so amazing. I was waiting for her inside, and Tony was upstairs waiting with everyone else including Tom's mum and dad. I was dressed in a long black dress with golden arms.

The ceremony went perfectly and so did the reception. I think I did well. The only thing was the miserable face Tony had on him because he could not have a drink until the wedding reception and that pissed him right off. Well, it all went exceptional. Everyone made speeches and I and Tom were presented with a beautiful bouquet of flowers and then the DJ took over and the drinking started getting in full swing. After a couple of hours, I had to take the children home and put them all to bed. I was knackered and fell asleep on the sofa. Morning arrived too quickly and I had a bloody hangover and as I was getting the kids dressed and giving them their breakfast, I got a phone call from my son. He had arranged a booking on the top floor of a pub in town for a wedding breakfast for everyone at 12 noon. Could not believe this. He knew I could pay for this as I had money and he didn't. What a fuckin wind-up merchant he was. He had taken over again. Bully boy in full swing. Well, I got the kids dressed nice and got a taxi to the pub, feeling like shit. We all arrived one by one and went upstairs to our private tables. Kelly and Tom, the bride and groom turned up, Kelly looking like crap, Tom not looking quite as rough. Well, when everyone turned up, we sat and ordered food and drink. Anyone could order what they wanted and boy! Did they go to town? There were steaks here and fish there and kids' meals everywhere and the wine and beer kept flowing.

Unbelievable, thanks to Mike but shit, a bit over the top. When all was done, I produced my card to pay and it was over £100 quid. A sharp intake of breath here from me but I paid for it all and everyone went home happy, except one didn't (TONY). What a fucking surprise. Everyone went home except him and he went off on his own to drink more. I thought I had done well and went home alone completely exhausted. I slept most of the day and evening but soon woke up when the drunken bum came in. He puked up in the bathroom and went straight to bed, thank God.

The next day was the last day before my brothers went back to the states and we all went to the train station in Nottingham to wave them off. I didn't know if I would ever see them again and that hurt me. Kelly and Tom hugged them and never wanted to let go.

Well, life settled down to nearly normal again. Kelly and Tom got on wonderfully and they were and still are in love. The children started growing up to be wonderful little human beings and they decorated this new rented house just how they wanted it. I said earlier that life settled down to nearly normal again, but it didn't for me with my other half. He carried on drinking, even after he had his sessions with the probation officer. He used to stay out all day and come home around teatime, then ended up just going to sleep on the sofa until bedtime. I was walking a bit better now, not using my stick but one time I had to get in touch with my consultant and tell him there was a little screw starting to poke through the skin on my ankle and it was hurting me. The hospital had me in again and I went for surgery and came home the day after with a couple of stitches in my ankle and the screw gone. I was told by the doctor that they could not remove any more screws as my leg would come apart from my foot. Well! That was a blow to my system and also, I would never walk properly again, always have a limp and would always have to wear flat shoes. I accepted that eventually but it was so hard.

With Tony's drinking, it got worse AGAIN. It was 2017. One day, Tony went out at 10 am and by 8 pm, there was no sign of him and I was starting to get very scared. I phoned my daughter up and asked what I should do and she told me to put a few clothes in a plastic bag and go get into a hotel in the city for a couple of days and stay there and she would take care of the rest. She was very fearful for my safety. I took her advice, raced around the flat taking my underwear and a couple of warm jumpers, got myself a taxi and went to the nearest hotel in town that I could find. You have no idea how much safer I felt. I knew in my heart that she would handle Tony for me because she had so much strength when it came to keeping me safe. In the morning, I phoned her and told her that I wanted him out forever so she told me to stay put and she would sort it. Well, she did. She went to the warden and told her he had to be evicted. His name was not on the rent book or the tenancy agreement so my warden went to the flat and told him to start packing as I was in fear of him yet again. She told him that he would be re-housed but not locally to me. I was not there so I don't know what his reaction was but on the second day of my stay in the hotel, I got a very quick phone call from my daughter telling me to get the bus home quick! As Tony had been taken to another town to look at a flat. I flew home with my carrier bag, let myself into the flat and had just turned my door key and locked myself in when the door handle moved and it was him. I HAD DONE IT! Hoo-fuckin-ray!

The warden came to speak to me and told me he was going to be re-homed and not near me but he could not take the flat unless he could move in with a bed. I just looked at my warden and said, 'Yes yes yes, let him have it.' I also just filled a plastic bag with underpants and socks and said I would go out for the day while he packed up all his stuff and the bed and just go. Kelly and her husband had hired a man with a van and by the end of the day, he had gone, his stuff had gone and the bed was gone. It just didn't bother me. I would just sleep on the sofa for a couple of days then go to the British Heart Foundation shop in town and buy myself a bed and that's what I did and I felt FREE! For the very first time in my life. I arranged the furniture to my liking and the knot of fear which was always in my stomach every day had gone. I got rid of all the pictures of him in my photo albums, all the photos in my phone, all the bits and pieces that he had left behind so that nothing at all remained of him! It has now been three years since I have been on my own and it feels fantastic.

I got myself a rescue cat and she came to me as an indoor cat when she was five years old. In 2019, my little friend got sick. Her name was Billie and I had to take her to the PDSA and was told she had gingivitis, a disease of the teeth and gums. I had to leave her at the cat hospital and they took most of her teeth out before I could bring her home. She was beautiful and very faithful and I had to buy her special food that wasn't lumpy so that she could eat her food more comfortably. Well, she was fine for a while, then her fur started looking shitty and she began having problems breathing. After a couple of days, she started going to the toilet outside of her box and lying under my heater in the living room, stretched out totally so that she could breathe. She could not eat or drink and literally went to skin and bone. I phoned the PDSA and they told me to bring her in straight away. She had contracted pyothorax which I was told it was where there was poison built up between the lungs and chest wall and was told the doctors were taking her straight in. She was desperately ill and they put her straight on drips and operated on her to insert a drain from her chest to the outside of her body. My heart ached for her but after her op, I was told I could visit her and take in some of her favourite food. I visited her every day and found her lying on her side with this tube coming from her side. I was crying but she recognised me straight away and I put a bit of her favourite fish soup on a little plate and held it under her nose. She started eating it almost straight away so I left a few packets with the vets there. After seven days in the vet's hospital, I was allowed to take her home, after the tube in her side was removed with pain medication and antibiotics and was told to take her back in a week for a check-up. I thought the staff were wonderful to her and made a sizeable donation every time I took her for a check-up.

Each time I took her back and was happy to find that she was putting on weight little by little. I was so happy with that because she was like a little comfort blanket to me. She never left my side at home and followed me around like a little dog. She was so desperate for love and cuddles and I gave her both and still do. She has climbing frames and beds all over the flat but makes sure she tells me when it's bedtime and sleeps by my side on my bed every night. I really was so happy and content that she loved me so much.

She is now eight years old and as fat as a little butterball and faithful more than any man I know. She is my company, my little friend who gets all the special food and love that she wants and I love the fact that I nursed her back to health when she nearly left me to go to cats' heaven. I would give any woman or young girl out there, who has been groomed, abused, mentally and physically like me, have the guts eventually to ask for help. Stop being afraid and get away from the pain that I suffered at the hands of the men I was with. I always tell my friends, now that I live alone, to get rid of the men that are hurting you and get a cat. It works wonders. Well, my little friend has been with me for three years nears now and it is now 2020. Although I have no internet or broadband and only have a mobile phone which I have had since 2013, I have finished going on my travels and my body is slowing down a bit, I keep walking and moving as much as possible and eat healthily. I am writing this story on a broken-down laptop and only have a printer. It has taken me nearly a year to write but I thought, before I finish with THE END, I was curious one day and went on Google and typed in my first love's name, not knowing what the outcome would be.

Well, I nearly dropped through the bloody floor when his name took me straight to Facebook and there he was. His picture looking straight at me. He was one year older than me, had a white beard, but longish hair and my heart jumped in my chest because looking at his face and into his eyes reminded me he was still my first and only ever sweetheart. It had been a few years but he hadn't changed one bit. There was a phone number with his picture and I sent him a message straight away. I never got a reply so quick in my life. He told me he would meet me the next evening and it was in February 2020 and he would meet me in our usual place just over the train lines in Netherfield and was surprised when I told him I lived alone.

Well, I raced up to the hairdressers to have my hair cut, tomboy style but it was still blonde, just like the old days. I was to meet him at 5 pm in the evening and it was so very cold but I made sure I put on my makeup, dressed for the cold and went to our street and waited. I think he was just as eager as I was. I was so nervous but finally, a big silver Jaguar car turned up and when I saw that he was alone, I suggested he come back to my flat. He parked up and we walked towards the lift to the 2nd floor. He stood at one side of the lift and I stood at the other and all of a sudden, he grabbed me to him and kissed me and do you know what? His kisses were still the same as when he was sixteen and if I had got some super glue with me, I would have glued my lips to his. We looked into each other's eyes and the spark was still very much there and had never left and he made my insides tingle with love and passion all at once. I have to be candid about this part of my story. Since I had separated from my second marriage, my first love Stephen has always known where I was in the area. He always happened to be parked up in a work's van somewhere in the area where he knew I would be, whether it be where I was shopping, or where I was walking. This was happening from when I was in my forties. If I saw him in his work's van, I would just climb in and off, we would go to find a quite spot, anywhere we could park up and have sex, a kiss, a cuddle and just go at it like rabbits. We even made love in the back of his van once which was full of rolled up carpets. It was uncomfortable but we didn't care as the passion was always there. We kept going like that for probably for 30 years, never stopping to breath when we were together. I must say though that I was never ever unfaithful to any of husbands until we were separated and not together anymore, but then, I was always on the move. Stephen and I lost touch with each other, but now I have found him again.

I took him home and we sat on the sofa just kissing and holding but before long, I led him to the bedroom and our clothes came off quicker than you could take a breath, and we were all over each other. He touched every part of my body, although I was fatter than from many years ago and I felt embarrassed about that, but my skin was soft, I had no wrinkles and he was the same. We made love passionately but we had to do it a little bit differently because he had kidney disease and diabetes and I was just a bit flabbier than he remembered me but we both had orgasms. YES! It does happen when you are old, and we just lay naked, side by side, breathless and staring at each other for the longest time. There were no words, just kisses and holding each other tight. I was crying with emotion and he just held me. Well, we did finally get dressed and go and cuddle on the sofa but he didn't have much time because he had to get back to his other wife. He told me that he didn't marry her because he loved her but out of convenience because she offered to bring up our three daughters. He also told me he didn't sleep in the same bedroom as her and had not had sex with her for at least ten years. I was gobsmacked but I believed him. He wanted to see me again but we had to devise a plan so that could happen.

Up until now, I have to go with his plans. It's either when he has to go to the hospital or when he goes out to an auction to buy antiques so I have to accept that and there are months between visits to me. I have to be patient and I must admit, the very first text I got from him was, "Just thought I would let you know that I have never stopped loving you." Every night since then I have always had a text saying, "Goodnight, I love you," and he phones me every day to talk to me and tells me he loves me.

From the age of fifteen when I had my first kiss from him, I knew he was the one and it has stayed with me all my life, and so it has with him. He has to plan when he can come to see me and I have to accept that but I do know that we will never lose track of each other again. My heart died the first time I abandoned my first love and family. It also died when I lost the father of my other two children from my second marriage but now my life has been revived once again because I have connected with my first love again, but I am still broken because I can never have him in my arms completely because he belongs to someone else so my heart is in two halves, but now we are old, I hope to connect with him again on our next journey together, but until then, we are really going to make the best of each other.

Now, my eyesight is failing, I am crippled and not in good health but he still accepts me for who I am, his first love.

Even if we can't be together, my love, I'm glad that you were part of my life, and by the way, my first love, thank you for putting another engagement ring and a wedding ring on my finger and also, the silver cross and heart around my neck. I have added only one thing, a sunflower pendant which contains your photo, your hair and a little of your blood. These are always with me and close to my heart for when we can't meet up. Don't cry because it's over, smile because it happened.

YOU ARE BORN, YOU LIVE AND YOU DIE, THEN YOU MOVE ON.
LOVE IS WONDERFUL BUT LIFE SUCKS.

THE END.

Epilogue

You can never make right your mistakes so don't try and go back into your memories to make things different and put things right. Just put the past behind you and live each day as if it were your last. This book I have written is dedicated to all my family. I want to mention Stephen, my first love at the age of 15 years, who gave me three wonderful daughters, Mandy, Cindy and Trudy. I thank you. To my second love, Steve, who gave me two amazing children, Michael and Kelly, one who does not like me very much, for reasons only he knows, and two more marriages, which I do not give a crap about, because at their hands, I was abused, mentally and physically and was almost murdered.

My first love said to me not so long ago, 'We must have had the longest affair in fucking history,' (his words, not mine) and yes, we still see each other whenever we get the chance, even as I bring this book to a close. People say to me that you never forget your very first kiss and your very first love – and it's true, we haven't. He is now 74 years old and I am 73 years old. We both have health issues but he never goes to sleep without sending me a message on my phone, just to say that he has never stopped loving me.

I live alone, waiting for the chance, day by day when I will get a little time with him and that does still happen, and then he has to leave and go back to his family, which includes our three daughters, but we have kept our love a secret for many years up until this day. I hope I pass away before him, then I won't have to shed any more tears on my pillow every night because I miss him when he leaves me to go back to his other home, and I won't have an empty space in my bed where he should be, holding me close to his body as we both fall asleep. I still have many regrets, and to this day, I have never forgiven myself for breaking his heart, so now at 73, my memories are as clear as if it all happened yesterday, but I will never forgive myself for what I did to him and the hurt that I caused in his heart, but I do know that we have always loved each other and always will but I will always remain **BROKEN!**

Afterword

How This Book Came to be Written

It was my daughter Kelly who really made this book happen. She was nine years old and I was still living with her dad and we were a family. One day she was in my bedroom, dancing around in some of my stage clothes which I had bought back from London and she turned to me and said, "Mum, you should write a story about your life."

"Maybe one day I will babe," I said just to pacify her at the time. Little did I know that a lot more things were to happen in both our lives before that was to happen. It was all put on hold for quite a few years before I finally put my life story to paper.

Kelly got involved with her first boyfriend when she was only 16 years old and as she stayed with him, he became violent and once even tried to set her on fire. That ended but not before she was physically and mentally damaged forever. She became mentally strong after that although, always with a smile on her face, she constantly suffered from inside but did not let demons get the better of her. She developed psoriasis all over her body due to mental stress but still smiled. Still telling me to write a book and still I kept putting her off. I crushed her spirit when I left her dad but still, she managed to smile and never stopped loving me.

To try and make her happy, when I lived alone in my first sheltered accommodation, I obtained a credit card and put myself in debt by taking her to Memphis in Tennessee where we stayed right across the highway from Graceland, Elvis Presley's home, in a place called Heartbreak Hotel. She was a great Elvis fan and I knew this would cheer her up. We stayed for eight days and spent most of our time on Beale Street where we feasted on corndogs, danced in the streets to the music and both had tattoos done. She still suffered from psoriasis and was at times quite aware of it. I was also there when she cut off all her hair and carried on. She has now, in her late thirties got arthritic psoriasis which has got into her bones now but she still soldiers on and still smiles and still tells me to write about my life. This girl of mine never thinks of herself and always puts others first. During the first lockdown, she dressed up as Barry the Bear and sang to all the old people who were in care homes in her village and mine. She was mentioned on the local news for doing things like that. She has a wonderful husband, Tom, who supports her in everything she does and when she feels ill, he is always by her side, helping with the children and watching over Kelly to make sure she is okay. He is her strength. When first lockdown came, Kelly phoned me and said, "Mum, get writing, now is your chance because I stayed at home too afraid to go out and that was the final push I needed."

Kelly, you are my hero.
Hazel Longley
1947–Present Day

THE END

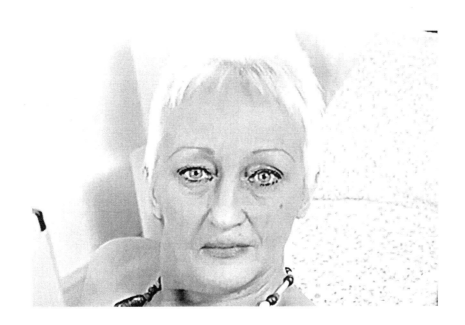

Me

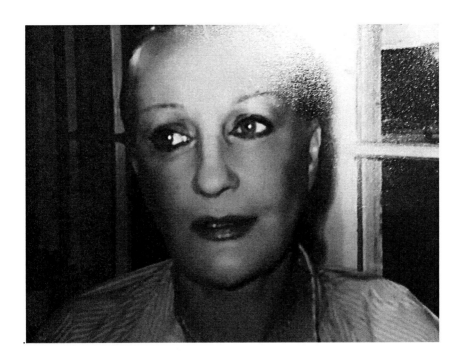

My birth mother from hell

Me